CULTURAL
REVOLUTION
IN BERLIN

CULTURAL REVOLUTION IN BERLIN

Jews in the age of Enlightenment

SHMUEL FEINER & NATALIE NAIMARK-GOLDBERG

Bodleian Library
UNIVERSITY OF OXFORD

JOURNAL of JEWISH STUDIES

First published in 2011 by

The Bodleian Library
Broad Street, Oxford OX1 3BG
www.bodleianbookshop.co.uk

in association with

Journal of Jewish Studies
Yarnton Manor, Yarnton
Oxford OX5 1PY
www.jjs-online.net

[Journal of Jewish Studies Supplement Series 1]

ISBN   978 1 85124 291 7
ISNN   0022–2097

Text © Journal of Jewish Studies, 2011

Images © Müller Library, Oxford Centre for Hebrew and Jewish Studies,
Oxford, except: Figures 4, 31, 56, 69 akg-images; Figures 7, 8 & 61B © Bodleian
Library, University of Oxford, 2011; Figure 10 Historische Museum, Hanover;
Figure 17 Beinecke Rare Book and Manuscript Library, Yale University.

Cover design by Dot Little
Text designed and typeset in 12 on 14 Monotype Fournier
by illuminati, Grosmont
Printed by Information Press, Eynsham, Oxford on 150 gsm Hello Matt

British Library Catalogue in Publishing Data
A CIP record of this publication is available from the British Library

Contents

Foreword

THE *Journal of Jewish Studies*, which appears under the ægis of the Oxford Centre for Hebrew and Jewish Studies, is delighted to launch its new series of supplements with a volume entitled *Cultural Revolution in Berlin* by Shmuel Feiner and Natalie Naimark-Goldberg. It is based on rare material held in the Müller Library at the Centre and enriched by sources from the Bodleian Library of Oxford University. We are very proud to release this book in association with Bodleian Library Publishing.

Cultural Revolution in Berlin is intended to serve as a concise guide to the eighteenth-century Jewish Enlightenment. It is aimed at general readers as well as at students in Jewish studies and modern history. The rare sources described in the book and available online at www.ochjs.ac.uk/mullerlibrary, together with the bibliography appended to the volume, will enable more advanced students to investigate in depth the original documents.

Journal of Jewish Studies

Preface

BERLIN and Jewish Enlightenment (the Haskalah) are familiar topics in modern Jewish history.

The embracing of the civil and rational values of eighteenth-century Europe by Jewish intellectuals connected to the Enlightenment circles in the Prussian capital brought about a cultural revolution within the traditional Jewish society of the day. The picture of this transformation is usually based upon data painstakingly collected from sources that are preserved in various libraries. The story here presented, however, is entirely based upon one collection held in the Leopold Müller Memorial Library of the Oxford Centre for Hebrew and Jewish Studies: the private library of the 'father of the *Wissenschaft des Judentums*' (The Science of Judaism), Leopold Zunz (1794–1886).

The creation of the Müller Library was simultaneous with that of the Oxford Centre for Postgraduate Hebrew Studies (now the Oxford Centre for Hebrew and Jewish Studies, a Recognized Independent Centre of the University of Oxford), which was founded in 1972. Over the decades the library acquired major collections through generous donations such as Getzel Kressel's library on the literature and the history of Palestine and Israel, Gedaliah Elkoshi's collection of Hebrew literature and Rabbi Dr Louis Jacobs's library on Rabbinic Judaism. A milestone in the library's history has been the acquisition of the book collection of the Montefiore Endowment, which was made possible by a munificent donation from the Foyle Foundation. The collection bears the name of Sir Moses Montefiore (1784–1885), the most famous Jew of nineteenth-century England. In 1869 he founded the Judith Montefiore Theological College in memory of his late wife, 'to promote the study and advancement of the

holy Law and general Hebrew literature'. Learned men were invited to teach at the College and the first principal was the eminent orientalist Louis Loewe. It is for this institution that a most remarkable library was accumulated. It reflects Montefiore's strong desire to promote Jewish integration into the wider society – this is probably why he earned the designation of the perfect Englishman. It was in this vein, but almost certainly beyond Sir Moses's own perspective, that the second principal of the College, Moses Gaster (1891–96), decided to acquire the private library of Leopold Zunz. This collection of one of the key scholarly figures in the nineteenth-century Science of Judaism, which contained the library of Lazarus Bendavid, one of the leaders of the radical Jewish Enlightenment in Berlin at the turn of the nineteenth century, transformed the Montefiore Library into a unique resource for the study of Haskalah.

The main emphasis in Zunz's collection is on eighteenth- and nineteenth-century history of the Jews in Europe, and their fight for emancipation and integration into wider society while retaining Jewish identity. Over 150 titles, many of them rare nineteenth-century pamphlets, relate to the legal position of Jews in various states, covering issues such as enfranchisement, judicial autonomy and the position of Jews vis-à-vis local and state authorities. In the many eulogies on the occasion of the enthronement or death of emperors, kings and princes the commitment of Jews to secular rulers comes unambiguously to the fore. Publications on Jewish institutions, such as annual reports of rabbinical schools, or works concerning education in general, shed light on the organization of Jewish communities in modern Europe. This remarkable collection also includes over fifty works by or on the Berlin Jewish philosopher Moses Mendelssohn (1729–1786), and the œuvre of Abraham Geiger (founder of the Hochschule für die Wissenschaft des Judentums), thus providing a comprehensive sketch of the religious, political and social history of the Jews in modern Europe and a precious insight into Leopold Zunz's own reading of the Jewish Enlightenment.

The story presented here originates from Professor Shmuel Feiner's stay at Yarnton in 2007 as a Visiting Fellow of the Oxford Centre for Hebrew and Jewish Studies. Feiner, the

author of the comprehensive study on *The Jewish Enlightenment* (2004), was impressed and excited by the unrivalled wealth of the Foyle–Montefiore Collection, and he suggested that Zunz's books and pamphlets would tell the story of the cultural revolution in Berlin, the intellectual home of the most outstanding representative of Jewish Enlightenment, Moses Mendelssohn, who figures prominently in the narrative. In this monograph Shmuel Feiner and Natalie Naimark-Goldberg lead the readers along the shelves of the Müller Library with a small excursion among the manuscripts of the Bodleian Library, thus opening up Oxford's unique resources for the study of modern Jewish history.

The publication is part of a larger project and was also designed as a companion to a conference on Jewish Enlightenment combined with an exhibition in the Bodleian Library in February 2011, for which some of the most important books from the Zunz Collection and the Bodleian Library had been selected. A lasting result of the project is the digital library of all the primary sources discussed in the book, which is accessible through the website of the library.

We are very grateful to the Foyle Foundation for its generous support to the project and to Milena Zeidler for her indispensable assistance in preparing the manuscript for publication.

Piet van Boxel
Hebrew Curator, Bodleian Libraries
Fellow Librarian, Oxford Centre for Hebrew and Jewish Studies

Jerusalem

---

oder

über religiöse Macht

und

Judenthum.

Von

Moses Mendelssohn.

Frankfurt und Leipzig,

1791.

CHAPTER I

The Haskalah Library in Oxford:
focus and limits of the story

AN IMPRESSIVE COLLECTION of books, pamphlets, treatises and letters, part of the Foyle–Montefiore collection and representing a significant part of modern Jewish history, is deposited at the Leopold Müller Memorial Library of the Oxford Centre for Hebrew and Jewish Studies in Yarnton. Having been collected over more than two centuries – from the times when Jews first began to acculturate and actively participate in non-Jewish society, until the emergence of Zionism and the years when Jews living in European countries were taking ever deeper roots in their places of residence – this collection gives clear testimony to the hopes and aspirations, the fears and frustrations, of the modernizing Jews, at least as seen by the Jewish bibliophiles who, throughout several generations, assembled a variety of works on Jews and Judaism published by Jews and gentiles in various European lands, mainly Germany and England.

Of the literary wealth deposited at the Leopold Müller Memorial Library and the Bodleian Library in Oxford, several dozen books and two manuscripts were selected to lead us on a journey through a decisive chapter in modern Jewish history, which as a cultural and social movement came to be known as the Haskalah, the Jewish Enlightenment.

From the early eighteenth until the end of the nineteenth century, relatively small groups of young maskilim (followers of the Jewish Enlightenment) from central and eastern Europe wrought a cultural revolution in the Ashkenazi Diaspora: the transfer of cultural sovereignty over Jewish public space into new hands. As a new intellectual elite, the maskilim set themselves up as educators, providing alternative ideological leadership in competition with the rabbinical, scholarly elite that thus far

(*opposite*) *Jerusalem or On Religious Power and Judaism* (1783), an exposition of Judaism in accordance with rational beliefs; Moses Mendelssohn's most influential work.

had held a complete monopoly over knowledge, books, values, education, supervision over norms and behaviour, and guidance of the public. The new elite wished for intellectual renewal and adopted some of the basic values of European Enlightenment culture, in particular humanism, religious tolerance, freedom of opinion, rationalism and the consciousness of progress. It took upon itself the responsibility for reforming traditional society in the light of these values.

Choosing the texts for this journey was no simple task, though the fact that there was room for 'selecting' attests to a rare luxury offered by this collection: few libraries in the world hold as many documents on this chapter of Jewish history as the library of the Oxford Centre for Hebrew and Jewish Studies, which is further complemented by the Bodleian collection of Hebrew books and manuscripts. The texts presented here were eventually selected because they help reconstruct important processes in the life of the Jewish community in central Europe, especially in the German lands, in the eighteenth century. While some of the texts enjoyed commercial success, not all of them were best-sellers at the time they appeared, and some had a very restricted readership. This applies in particular to the two manuscripts that never reached the printing press. Still, they serve to illuminate the cultural revolution among Ashkenazi Jewry brought about by the Haskalah.

The journey through these modest-looking, often even un-attractive books reveals a modern Jewish republic of letters. A new Jewish library emerged with them, transforming the long-standing balance of power in the Jewish community, and undermining the cultural supremacy of the rabbinic elite. Here we encounter a new type of Jewish intellectual, concerned not solely with religious matters as the traditional type of Jewish intellectual had been (and still was), but with educating the public according to modern ideals, and promoting alternative options for Jewish life in their lands of residence. The selected texts thus illustrate the emergence of a Jewish parallel to a phe-nomenon that was new in modern culture and was becoming ever stronger in European life – a sphere of public debate and public opinion. Some of the texts here selected illuminate yet

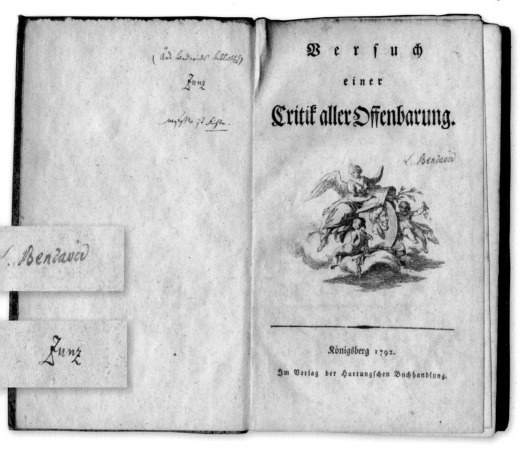

another phenomenon, also new in Ashkenazi Jewry and closely related to the Haskalah: the participation of Jewish intellectuals in the European public sphere.

The Haskalah is now known to be a multifaceted movement, articulated in many different ways in the many different settings where Jews lived. Perhaps the most prominent setting in which the movement came to the fore is Berlin. To be sure, there were other versions of the European Jewish Enlightenment which developed in various places such as Prague, London and Amsterdam, and later, until the end of the nineteenth century, also in many Jewish communities in eastern Europe. The varying geographical–cultural contexts had a decisive influence on the nature of the Enlightenment as manifested among Jews in different places. These significant trends have been discussed by

FIGURE I
Lazarus Bendavid's and Leopold Zunz's signatures in a book from the Foyle–Montefiore collection in Yarnton, Fichte's *Versuch einer Critik aller Offenbarung* (Attempt at a Critique of all Revelation) of 1792.

scholars in the field, who emphasized their singularity especially vis-à-vis the 'Berlin Enlightenment', and will not be considered here. Although the Haskalah neither started in Berlin nor took place only within its confines, at the time of its apogee the Prussian capital was its indisputable centre, physically and, perhaps even more so, ideologically. Berlin was the city every maskil sought to visit; it was the city where the first modern Jewish school was founded in 1778 ('The Free School') with the explicit goal of instilling maskilic ideals in the new generation; it was the city where a maskilic publishing house was established in 1784 ('The Oriental Press'), printing the largest number of maskilic publications produced anywhere; it was also the city that hosted the towering figure of Moses Mendelssohn (1729–1786), probably the most famous Jew in the eighteenth century. It was in Berlin where Mendelssohn resided, surrounded by an admiring circle of enlightened Jews, the city where he became the German Socrates.

The centrality of Berlin in our story derives from yet another, more pragmatic, ground: the fact that it was Lazarus Bendavid (1761–1832), a central figure among the maskilim in Berlin and Vienna around 1800, who established the basis for what eventually became the Yarnton collection, and that it was Leopold Zunz (1794–1886), the famous nineteenth-century Jewish scholar active in Berlin, who inherited his library and expanded it, before it was acquired by the scholar and rabbi Moses Gaster (1856–1939) when principal of the Judith Lady Montefiore College (1890–96). The collection reflects, to a significant extent, the interests and the world-view of the collectors and is representative of what was to be found in their private libraries.

The origins of this collection are also indicative of the central role that Moses Mendelssohn occupied in it. One could argue that this prolific writer who resided in Berlin is perhaps somewhat over-represented, not only through the works he himself published but also through the texts that were addressed to him – for example, *Heman über die Unsterblichkeit der Seele nach mosaischen Grundsätzen, in drey Gesprächen* (Heman on the immortality of the soul according to Mosaic principles in three

conversations), or which dealt with his life and thought, as for instance *Gedanken über Mosis Mendelssohns Jerusalem, in so fern diese Schrift dem Christenthum entgegen gesetzt ist* (Thoughts about Moses Mendelssohn's *Jerusalem*, in so far as this writing opposes Christianity). Nonetheless the collections at the Yarnton and Bodleian libraries make us realize what a strong impression Mendelssohn made on the minds of German Jews throughout the modern period. But they also help us place him in a historical perspective, as part of a broader effort to renew Jewish culture, to widen its scope and to put an end to Jewish intellectual isolation. As the selection presented here makes clear, in order to understand the appearance of the modern Jewish republic of letters, of the modern Jewish intellectual, it is necessary to pay attention to processes that extended for decades before Mendelssohn appeared on the public stage and continued after his death.

FIGURE 2
Heman über die Unsterblichkeit der Seele nach mosaischen Grundsätzen (1773), was dedicated to Mendelssohn, as stated on its title page.

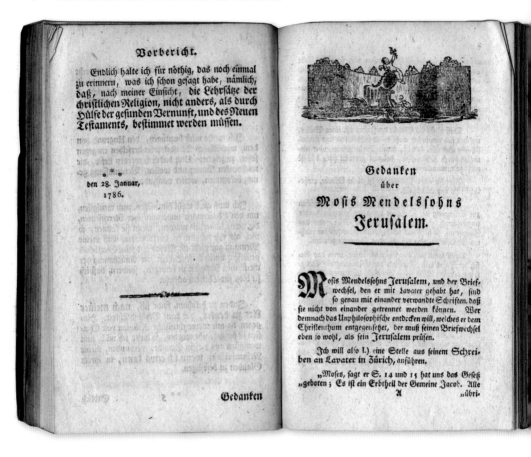

FIGURE 3
Gedanken über Mosis Mendelssohns Jerusalem, in so fern diese Schrift dem Christenthum entgegen gesetzet ist, a book discussing Mendelssohn's famous work *Jerusalem*, published anonymously immediately after his death.

As stated, the collection does not present a comprehensive story of the Haskalah. Significantly under-represented are expressions of this movement in other places where it developed, such as in the Habsburg Empire and in the eastern parts of Europe, mainly Galicia and Russia, in the nineteenth century. Nor is it to be seen in any sense as the story of the modernization of 'the Jews' in general, much as it illuminates an important trend within Jewry. For one thing, women are conspicuously absent. The story of Jewish women's modernization, at least at this point, runs along a different track, not necessarily apart from the Enlightenment, but not in the paths traced below either. The Haskalah as a movement alienated women, not only as producers of maskilic texts but also as an audience. The scant number of women who ventured along the path of

the modern, secular intellectual in the waning years of the eighteenth century and in the first decades of the nineteenth century moved on a different course, that of the European Enlightenment and the European public sphere, which surely did not encourage women to adopt a public voice, but neither did it seal off hermetically their participation. On this path stepped Mendelssohn's own daughter, Dorothea Mendelssohn-Veit-Schlegel (1764–1839), who was active as a writer and translator but never in the Jewish realm; so too did Esther Gad (1767?–1830s), a Jewish author from Breslau who, with the exception of one maskilic poem, addressed all of her works to a German and English public.

Neither does our depiction of the Haskalah tell the story of Sephardic Jews living in European lands, who had long maintained much closer contact with their surrounding cultures. Sephardic Jews did not need to go through the same processes and struggles as their Ashkenazi brethren in order to read a non-Jewish or non-religious book, to approach the sciences or to master the vernacular. It is therefore the great cultural transformation that took place specifically in Ashkenazi communities in central Europe that stands at the centre of this narrative, and that traces the main development of the Haskalah from its moderate and scattered beginnings in the early 1700s, through the height of the movement in the second half of the eighteenth century, until its final stage around 1800. By then, maskilic ideals among German Jews were receding and making space for new movements and ideologies.

FIGURE 4
Dorothea
Mendelssohn
(daughter of Moses
Mendelssohn), a
Jewish writer and
translator. Pastel
drawing, 1798.

CHAPTER 2

The early maskilim and the renewal of Jewish culture

THE HASKALAH became known as one of the most significant movements in modern Jewish history. But there was not really much at its outset to augur the sweeping changes in Jewish society it would promote, the great secular revolution it would instigate, or the fierce combats between its future leadership and the traditional religious elite that would stem from it. It started as a much more moderate effort towards cultural renovation, launched by the curiosity and a passion for knowledge and philosophy that awoke among several young men in eighteenth-century central Europe – men who could not find intellectual satisfaction within the boundaries of the institutions, knowledge and libraries of the religious elite, in which they had been reared.

The impulse towards intellectual renewal among these young scholars was largely motivated by a sense of cultural inferiority. The early maskilim believed a wide gap separated them intellectually from their more broadly educated European contemporaries. Europe had advanced and Jews were being left behind with a sense of inferiority and frustration. Throughout maskilic texts, writers bemoan the Jewish fall from intellectual glory; the maskilim considered it a historical fact that ancient Judaism was the source of the sciences and that it was the Jews who had brought knowledge to the world. How did it happen that it was precisely we, members of the Jewish people (they asked themselves and their contemporaries) who had once blessed the world with knowledge, but now lag behind the rest of humanity? How is it that we are now mocked by the gentiles on account of our ignorance?

It is the purported cultural backwardness of the Jews as a collective that the early maskilim endeavoured to address.

FIGURE 5
Tobias Cohen, author of *Ma'aseh Tuviyah* (The Work of Tobiah), a popular compendium of medicine and natural philosophy, first published in 1707.

Presenting themselves as 'redeemers' of knowledge, they engaged in the study of what they considered external sciences as well as of those fields that were indigenous to Jewish culture but had been disregarded for a long time. Since the objective was to satisfy their own curiosity, but no less than that to expand the cultural world of their fellow Jews, and also to improve the image of the Jewish minority in the eyes of the gentiles, they started to produce a corpus of texts in Hebrew dealing with various fields that were conspicuously absent from the pre-modern Ashkenazi Jewish library, acting independently, not yet as coordinated members of a movement. Works on science (astronomy, mathematics, medicine and geography), philosophy and ethics, Hebrew language and Hebrew grammar thus steadily began to enrich and diversify the book supply accessible to Jewish readers.

Reclaiming 'external' knowledge: secular motivations, religious justifications

The mission of 'redeeming' knowledge and widening the cultural scope of the Jews proved no easy task, especially since the subject of study was characterized in Ashkenazi culture, following the Talmudic tradition, as 'external' *hokhmot* – forbidden extra-Jewish and extra-religious knowledge. The challenges confronted by the early maskilim are illuminated by an early attempt to bring up-to-date knowledge to a Jewish audience as contained in a manuscript by Meir ben Judah Loeb Neumark (apparently born in 1688), preserved in the Bodleian Library. The manuscript, entitled *Tokhen ha-kadur* (Order of the Sphere), was part of David Oppenheimer's library from the beginning of the eighteenth century. Oppenheimer (1664–1736), born in Worms, was chief rabbi of Moravia and Prague. He was also a collector of books almost to the point of obsession, who accumulated an extensive library, which was acquired by the Bodleian Library almost a century after his death and which today forms the core of its Hebrew manuscripts collection. During his lifetime Oppenheimer was known for inviting Jewish students to profit from his impressive library, providing

FIGURE 6
Rabbi David Oppenheimer, owner of an extensive library and patron of Jewish scholars.

:ספר:

:תוכן: :הכדור:

ביאור איכות וכמות כדור הארץ תוכן כדור גלגל נטושים עליו

ארבעת היסודות ארץ והטבעות מחוצר היא החכמה

המכונת בעיניהם קוסמוגראפיאה ידיעת

העולה וכל דבר ועבר עליו תעלומה

כן רוחות איתני שרקמת ולכות

דרכי כנשרלות תאמצין

וטרלוש הארץ רען

וגוראת בוראם

יעשו

העתיקו מלשון אלמנייא ללשונינו הקדושה הבחור הורם במושכלות מעם זולתו

שאיר בן לאדוני אבי מורי׳ יהודא ליב נ׳׳שמ הענא קצושיינים
יהודא בערלן

ועף הסופת ...... חצות אלקים .... גביא/ ...... לאון
שם .... אחרי ....
ולאנוש ...... :

FIGURES 7 & 8
(*preceding pages*)
Tokhen ha-kadur
by Meir Neumark:
frontispiece added to
the 1703 manuscript
during the lifetime of
David Oppenheimer
(*left*); and title page of
the manuscript (*right*).

them with the necessary support to devote their time to learning. Meir Neumark, son of a printer from Berlin and the author of *Tokhen ha-kadur*, was one of the young, promising scholars who enjoyed Oppenheimer's patronage. Urged by this rabbi and motivated by a will to make his Jewish co-religionists acquainted with the latest scientific and geographical discoveries, Neumark took the unusual step of turning to German and possibly Latin texts and the yet more uncommon step of trying to make their content accessible to a Jewish audience by rendering them into Hebrew. *Tokhen ha-kadur* is the result of such an effort.

The case of Neumark illuminates how remarkable an intellectual achievement it was to produce a scientific text for a Jewish audience in the early eighteenth century. Like other Jewish authors engaged in a similar task, he had to overcome linguistic and ideological barriers that stood in his way. Linguistically, German and, above all, Latin – the languages of the sciences, from which Neumark translated his text – were largely unknown to most Jews. Latin was learned through classical education and employed in the Church and the universities, which were almost completely inaccessible to Jews. German was rarely used by Jews in their daily lives, for although they lived in German-speaking countries their means of communication among themselves was a western form of Yiddish rather than the vernacular German. But even the target language, Hebrew, was problematic, as it hardly lent itself to the task. Although as Talmudic scholars they certainly mastered Hebrew, the whole terminology needed in order to express modern ideas and scientific concepts was a challenge strongly felt by Neumark, as it was by all the maskilim who took upon themselves a similar mission throughout the eighteenth century (and to some extent remained so even as late as the early twentieth century). This difficulty in the use of Hebrew for dealing with sciences and non-religious subjects in general is clearly reflected once again by the fact that Neumark and other maskilim introduced new (or at least not well known) Hebrew words to express new concepts accompanied by German or Latin translation in order to clarify their meaning.

Beyond the practical difficulty in the use of language, the ideological obstacle they confronted may have been even more formidable and difficult to overcome. A central question, unique to the Jewish context and not confronted by other European enlighteners, was whether it was legitimate to introduce secular knowledge into Jewish culture. The sciences were largely perceived at the time as forbidden fields, and Jews who devoted effort to their study had to cope both with the

FIGURE 9
Nehmad ve-na'im, a seventeenth-century work on science first published in 1743.

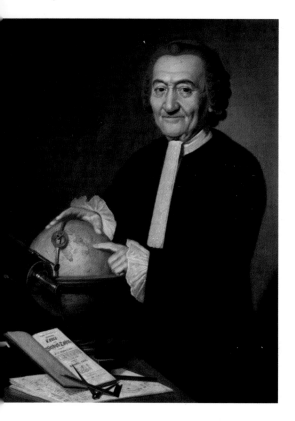

FIGURE 10
Raphael Levi of
Hanover, depicted
as a typical
eighteenth-century
scholar in European
garb, surrounded
by the symbols of
science at the time
such as measuring
instruments, a globe,
a telescope, writing
utensils and science
books.

danger of being condemned by society and with their own fear of undermining their religious faith. They had to justify their daring acts and innovative claims, sometimes having to resort to artful formulations.

The most common way to legitimize the introduction of 'foreign' knowledge to a Jewish audience and to make the ideological barrier less dramatic for both authors and readers of scientific texts was to present them as serving religious purposes. The fulfilment of a central commandment in Judaism, the consecration of the new month, with the attendant need to calculate the exact time of the beginning of the new month, served as a main reason (or excuse) to turn to outside sources and bring updated knowledge of astronomy, mathematics, geometry and even geography to a Jewish audience. This justification, which made it easier to find a readership among Jews, appears in many of the scientific books published in Hebrew throughout the eighteenth century. A text such as *Nehmad ve-na'im* (Delightful and Pleasant) stressed this argument on its title page, even though more than as a religious work it is to be seen as a comprehensive compendium on astronomy and geography that introduced Jewish readers to modern scientific discoveries and inventions. Finished in 1613 in Prague by David Gans (1541–1613) – a Jewish astronomer and historian, student of scientists Johannes Kepler and Tycho Brahe, and disciple of Moses Isserles and the Maharal, two eminent rabbis who encouraged scientific study – this book had remained in manuscript form and was published in 1743 for the first time, as part of the efforts by early maskilim to disseminate the sciences, though perhaps also to show the existence of a Jewish scientific tradition and thus nurture Jewish pride.

Another example of such a work came from the pen of Raphael Levi of Hanover (1685–1779). Levi, a Jewish philosopher and man of science who worked as a teacher of mathematics and astronomy, gathered around him a circle of students and admirers. He was encouraged in his investigations and publications by religious motivation: to help better fulfil the Commandments, for instance, by presenting astronomical calculations and time-tables for the sanctification of the new month as in *Luhot ha-'ibur* (Tables of Intercalation) (Leiden 1756 and Hanover 1757), two of his Hebrew astronomy books, and, no less than that, to comprehend the greatness of God and His creation through the knowledge of astronomy.

Along with this strong religious belief, Levi was fully committed to Enlightenment and science, and he viewed himself as a scientist, as shown by his portrait in which he appears as a typical eighteenth-century scholar. The pursuit of science brought this observant Jew into contact not only with non-Jewish knowledge but also with non-Jewish intellectuals. It is noteworthy that he was able to develop his scholarship and expand his scientific and philosophical knowledge by spending several years living in the home of the famed German philosopher and father of calculus, G.W. Leibniz (1646–1716).

FIGURE 11
Ma'amar ha-Torah veha-hokhmah, Mordechai Gumpel Schnaber's Hebrew science book (1771).

In the second half of the eighteenth century, the encounter with the sciences led to varying positions within the Haskalah. From among the early maskilim, some adhered to quite subversive rationalist standpoints, including Mordechai Gumpel Schnaber (1741–1797), a Berlin-born medical student in London who published in 1771 an up-to-date science book in Hebrew entitled *Ma'amar ha-Torah veha-hokhmah* (A Dissertation on the Law and Science). In it Schnaber (also known as George Levison in the English works he wrote)

FIGURE 12
Yesod 'olam, a medieval Hebrew work on astronomy, reprinted by Barukh Schick of Shklov in 1777 as part of his untiring efforts to disseminate scientific knowledge among his co-religionists in eastern Europe.

ventured to defend the new science in general and Copernicus's and Newton's theories in particular. Others, like Barukh Schick of Shklov (1744–1808), argued vehemently for the importance of the study of sciences but never transcended traditional boundaries. An ordained rabbi and member of a prestigious rabbinic family, Schick came to Berlin in 1777, where he spent almost a year and frequented the circles of the maskilim there before returning to his native Byelorussia, much affected by the intellectual ferment in Berlin. He acted vigorously to spread scientific knowledge among Jews in eastern Europe, producing numerous publications on anatomy, astronomy, geometry and mathematics, one of the earliest being a new edition of *Yesod 'olam* (Foundation of the Earth), a classic of medieval Hebrew astronomy. However, his religious commitment remained untouched and all along he continued to embrace a traditional stance.

Reviving the Hebrew language

The early maskilim were not only greatly disturbed by the neglect of the sciences, considered an external realm; they equally decried the pitiful decay of the Hebrew language. The study of Hebrew, so they claimed, had been neglected by many generations of Talmudic scholars, who showed no interest in this discipline. Though they obviously learned the holy tongue as part of their religious studies, the interest in developing and understanding the mechanics of the language was missing, as the errors that abounded in contemporary Hebrew texts testified. Contrary to the secondary place of Hebrew in the traditional curriculum of their time, the early maskilim imputed to the 'wisdom of grammar' immense significance. Moreover, the proper knowledge of Hebrew was considered essential for the refinement of Jewish culture and philosophy: it was an indispensable tool for clarifying and purifying the Bible, which was seen as the basis for understanding the very origins of language.

Among those who promoted the study of Hebrew and significantly enriched and renovated the Jewish library with books on Hebrew grammar and language, Shlomo Zalman Hanau (1687–1746) occupied a prominent place. Hanau, a travelling scholar, and author of numerous works focusing on the Hebrew language, took it upon himself to correct the rampant errors that had crept into the study of Hebrew. Already in the earliest book he authored in 1708, *Binyan Shelomo* (Solomon's Building), composed when he was only 21 years of age, Hanau daringly condemned the grammatical ignorance prevalent among fellow

FIGURE 13
Shlomo Hanau's earliest work on Hebrew grammar, *Binyan Shelomo*, from 1724 (first published in 1708).

ספר

צוהר התיבה

עם מכסה התיבה

ספר נחמד מעט הכמות ורב האיכות כולל כל חכמת הדקדוק להפיק רצון
התלמידים לחבק ולהשכיל ללמוד וללמד כי כח מיוסד על התחלות
ראשינות המולידות מושכלים שניים דבר דבור על אפניו ע"פ מוהכים והקשים
מפאת החקירה הטבעית יסדי הבינו נס חקרו אים שמו נודע נשערים ה"ה
המדקדק הגדול הקורני נח' ומו"ר שלמה הכהן נקרא זלמן העגנא בעל נכין שלמה
בכהת"ר יהודה ליב ס"ט זלה"ה :

ואלה מוסיף על הראשונים נכמה מעלות עובית שנחחדשו בו הנה"ת
מכ"י המחנר ה"ג' • וכל אחד כל מקומו סדרנו • וזה לך
האות אשר עשידנו • שני חלאי לבנה • ראה זה דבר חדש • ואם נט זאת
שאות י"ב וי"ג בקיטו' השמים המט מחוסרי הכנה ורני ירכשן להבינו ולא ימלא'נ'
וכדי להקל על המעיין הולגנו מעבד . לדף השער בגהבת המחבר מה שהעתקנו
מספרי קורי עטביש שם האריך למעניהו כדי לכבין אמריו כי נעפוונס הונה
בעוין נמרדזונהשנאמ' פרטיות כאט' ירא ה המעיין ואם זה לעומת העונרים
ונרדכנו פעמי' :

בריהרנפורט

תחת ממשלת האהרון החכם החסיד קינגליכר פרייסישר וירקליכר
גהיימט עטטש קריגש אונד דירעגירונדר מיניסטר איבר דיא
שלעזישי לאנדי ריהבור דעם שווארצין אדלו' ארדענס האך נבאהרנעה
גראף פאן האיום עקסעלענץ :

בדפוס ה"ה ר' יחיאל מיכל מייא מ"ס בברעסלא

לפ"ק   מכסה התיבה

Jews, including commentators and rabbis, that had led, in his view, to a deplorable misinterpretation of the Scriptures and to a shameful misreading of the liturgy. Hanau's harsh criticism met with protests by the spokesmen of the rabbinical elite, and he was forced to apologize for his audacious comments. Yet his arguments would find many sympathizers among later maskilim – first and foremost his famous student Hartwig Wessely (1725–1805), who would make this emphasis on Hebrew and on linguistic study a central endeavour. The enormous and long-lasting popularity of Hanau's work *Tsohar ha-tevah* (The Window of the Ark/Word), printed in Dyhernfurth in 1733, is indicative of the numerous followers he had throughout the eighteenth century.

Rational thinking and religious belief

In addition to the reclaiming of the sciences and the renaissance of the Hebrew language, the early maskilim also called for the revival of the philosophical tradition, largely ignored in Ashkenazi pre-modern culture. Influenced by rationalistic views expressed in the general Enlightenment, they reprinted medieval works on Jewish philosophy and ethics that had been absent from the Jewish library. The most notable event of this kind was undoubtedly the republication of *The Guide for the Perplexed*, Maimonides's celebrated philosophical work, which appeared in Jessnitz in 1742 after having been out of print for almost two centuries.

The early maskilim insisted on the pre-eminence of reason as expressed in Maimonides's work and opposed widespread trends within contemporary Judaism, notably superstition and Kabbalah, the ecstatic pietism of the messianic movement of Sabbatianism and the enthusiasm of Hasidism, the pietistic-kabbalistic movement that began to consolidate itself in eastern Europe in the last quarter of the eighteenth century. As committed Jews they encountered yet another challenge to tackle within eighteenth-century Jewry: the religious scepticism and the heretical trends that were spreading in the age of Enlightenment.

בתורה · לא בדמיון החושים · ולא בדעות שאנשים · ההולכים
נחשים · כי התורה והאמונה אינם מופלים כפי החוש והרעיון ·
קבלה והחזיון · אך השכל והמוסר המה בעלי הגיון · להורות
אל האדם את הנסיון · במשל ודמיון · כפי ענין הענין :

דך חושי הלא אדונינו · יחן את שבתו בתוכנו · והוא יספות
בצדק את דבריהו · וחלילה לי מעשות כדבר זה · לדלות
ואיך כפ'ל וגלוי עינים · ידבר על לבא הסמים · ואיך איש
כמוני ידבר באלהים · שהכל לפניו דוסים וזסים :

ה אחי הגיחי את האיש מדברי · ויקרא את שמו עיר"א היער"י ·
לאמר זה היהי מרפא ורני · לכל איש עברי אשר הלך עם בני מדי ·
סיערי · וסן כעיר פרח חדש יולד באדמס · כלי תורה וחכמה · אך
והמוזימס · אם יוריחו את התורה התמימה · וחכמה ומוסר טעמה ·
אן עלה יעלה האיש מאפל מצבו · וחאלקים ידברו :

מר חושי לעיר"א היער"י · את המכתב ולשון עברי : וסדר קבולי
המלות · ברב חבלות · ואת החפלות · לאל גורא עלילות ·
ואיש המדברי · הגליח והשכיל ועשה פרי :

ף אתי ללמד את תיראא היערים · חכמת ומוסרים · מליצות
וגדרים · תורה ומלות וחקים ישרים · וה' נתן חכמה · לאיש
שהיה בכתמה · עד שהשיג למפלה רמה · באחד מהמה :
בשנה הפליסית לנלאחם מהרו"ן · בסבחס על הר מרו"ן · ויבא
אליהס אחי ט'וב · מארן סו"ב · וגידרו חגדרת הישועס · מאיש
וסמו חביע'זר · ב'ן אל"י סו'ר · והאברת · דברי סלום ואמת ·
לאחי הגתי ולכל המחברת · רב לכס סבת במדבר סממה · בלא
לא לחס ולא סלמה · לא חורה ולא חכמה · פכו וסעו לכס דרך סר
'י · אל בני הפליס · אסר בירחא'ה סלימ'ה · וסס הסעיר מיוס ה' סמס ·
יתי לך ביתנאמן · בתוך עסלא אלמן · כ'ד אל"י סו'ר בי'ו'נסד'וי
חו'ר החונה באו'ר הבהיר :

מח אתי סניתי · ויאמר ברוך ה' מחסי ומלודתי · אשר פקד את
ביתי · לתת לחס בבית לחס יסודא · לתורה ולתעודה ·
אתי לאח"י סו'ב לסלוס · ויאמר · האס עוד באלרלות · חרפות
מאנסי הכפי'רה ונגאו'ה · אחי ח'י בנו'ד וחאו'ה · ויטן לח"י סו'ב
מתי מספר לער יחבון · קלחס לסתנעו · וקלחס מדת יצאו · וקלחס
לחס באו · בין כך · וצין כך · נחבדו וגופו · ויאמר אח"י סניתי כן
יאבדו כל אסר מדרך אמת תעו :

קך לאור ליסריס · ויקומו הנגברים · ויסעו מסוכו"ת ויחמר
בקרי'ת יערי'ס · ומסם נסעו לחיי הפעברי'ס · ויבא
מחכימה

יהיו סבלים כקופים · בהשמ'יס וסע'ולם · ובכפש ולורה וגולם · ו
ומדות · קנו עשר ידות · במראה ולא כתידות · והתבוננו במעשי ס
בכל מה שבפעולמו ברא · ועל הכל שם חו'שי את עיו'נו · וח'תי הג
עליהם את הגין'נו · וכתנו שבח ליונר בראשית · אשר ברא
ביום ס שבת :

ויהי היום ויצאו ללקט חרת ופקעת השדה למחייהם · וירחו
והנה איש עמד בסלונתס · פרוס מלבום · ולא בוש · ויתלום מ
הרפובים · אשר למחכל האדס טובים · ויחפור אחרי הפרשים ועיי
אשר למזג האנוסי יקריס' · וכראות האיש פרח את סניהס · ויברח מ
ויתחבא בתוך היער' · כדרך איש בער · ויפשיטו את בגדיהם גם ה
ופרוס נפלו כל היום שמה · עד כי בא האדס פרח כבשמך · אל המק
עמד שמה · לחפור אחרי שרסי האדמה · וילך את' יוידא אליו במחזה
לו רמיזה · ויבא האיש אליו · ויעמד לפגיו' · ויתנו לו את" מלר
וילעס סאוכל למו' · כח עשה החכס עמו · עד כי האדס פרח · הלך
בעגל אחרי הפריס' ויקחו אותו האהלה אשר שם סניהס' והוח עומר ס
ואכל עמהס · ובחר להסתותף בכל אהליהם :

ויאמר חוסי סערלכי עתה ילוס אלינו האיש כזה לעבוד ולסדר
ובוקר ונהריס · לחסוב עליס ולשאוב מיס· והמלאכה הי

ויען אתיויהמר לא טובה ענת חוש'יזאת הפעס · ליקח איש נכרי
מעס · ואם העני הזה בא להספתפח בנחלתינו · לא נגרשנו ב
ולא נקחהו לעבד לגו · אך לבי חושב ודעתי נומר' · לעשות מיליד ח
דבם תמר · ולהוליח מתוק ממר' · ומן הסלע הזה הוליא מיס' · לאל
העניס. עיני עבריס העוריס · אשר מאנו לכת בדרכי היסריס·
אעשה לרי · מאים המדברי' · לתבום בו את העברי' · אשר הלך בר
עס'ס'לורי : וכהמולי את בשר ערלת לבבו · נגילה ונשמחה בו ·
האיש הזה למופת · אל אנשי התופת' · אשר בין ג'את ובין סינס ·
כתאיסוחינס · בראותם אדס פרח · את חלקיס ירא' · ולומד מד
בחכמה ובמוסר מדבר · ובזה חולי יגהה את יחזרס ויתבע את מכ
ויהי רפואת תפלה למסובחם וחפצאחס :

ויאמר חוסי כמה לברך טובים · אל האמת והיסר המה קרובים
לא באנו אל המדבר · כ'אלעשות זה הדבר' · מפרו
משכיל וחבר · כבר קיימנו את העולם · כאחד הגדולים · וברוך ה
הקרה לפגינו כזאת · וזה לנו לטובה אות · ואתה חבי · חור עיני ולבב
עלי בתשהך · כדת מה לעשות את הנער כיולד והנני עבדך

ויאמר אתיוהגיתי · קח כא את האיש האיש אתי · ולמדתו כתב אשורית
עברית' · והורסו בחכמה ובידעה · לעבוד את הנו
ככתוב

FIGURE 15
(*preceding pages*)
The depiction of Ira
Ha-Ye'ari, a 'noble
savage' turned
by two maskilim
into Hurwitz's
utopian image of
the enlightened but
believing Jew.

In their self-perceived role as modern intellectuals, they strove to correct what they considered as the deplorable status of religion and morality, and with this purpose in mind they approached enlightened ideas not in order to erode the Jewish faith, as many feared, but, on the contrary, to reinforce Judaism and cultivate a better kind of Jew.

One such work that sought to combine reason and Enlightenment with religion and faith was *'Amude bet Yehudah* (Pillars of the House of Judah), published in 1766 by Judah Hurwitz (1734–1797), a Jewish doctor from Vilnius. Hurwitz identified two dangers which in his opinion were a menace to Judaism: kabbalistic mysticism on the one hand; radical philosophy or atheism on the other. In order to promote the ideal of an enlightened but devout Jew he employed the image of none other than the 'noble savage', a popular figure in European literature throughout the eighteenth century, represented in his work by Ira Ha-Ye'ari, a literary character strikingly similar to Man Friday in Daniel Defoe's *Robinson Crusoe*. The image of this primitive, simple man, uncorrupted by civilization, is surprisingly adapted to a Jewish context: in Hurwitz's version the savage is led by two maskilim on his path to Judaism, passing only through study and rational persuasion, proving that it was possible to soundly educate a natural man and to mould him into an educated, believing Jew by means of knowledge and reason without years of traditional Jewish study.

Some of Hurwitz's readers failed to understand the complex approach he employed in his book, which involved the use of sceptical arguments to support an orthodox position, and suspicions were raised of his being a heretic. In fact, his work is representative of a conservative stream of Jewish Enlightenment. Hurwitz favoured change, but in a gradual way, and, most importantly, without discarding old structures, first and foremost religion. Working mostly within a Jewish sphere, in Hebrew, he embodied a unique type of Jewish intellectual, one who was versed at one and the same time in Jewish traditional texts and modern science and philosophy, in Hebrew and in European languages, and wished to embrace modernity whilst retaining tradition.

CHAPTER 3

A modern Jewish intellectual: Moses Mendelssohn in Berlin

IT WAS only several decades after the beginning of the activity of the early maskilim that the figure of Moses Mendelssohn emerged in Berlin. The man who in time would be perceived as the paragon of the modern Jewish intellectual made his first scholarly steps in the circles of the early maskilim, though he would bring the Haskalah and Jewish involvement in non-Jewish culture to unprecedented heights.

As a young Torah student of 14, Mendelssohn, son of a Jewish scribe, had moved from his native Dessau to Berlin in 1743 following his teacher, David Fränkel, who had been appointed to head the rabbinate there. In close connection with the early Haskalah, Mendelssohn underwent a gradual change that transformed him from a Torah student of the traditional style to the illustrious philosopher he eventually became. In the Prussian capital, which was then under the rule of Frederick the Great (1712–1786) and had a Jewish community of 2,500–3,000 members, he made the acquaintance of early maskilim, among them Israel Zamość, native of Galicia, who had been involved in reprinting and commentating on classical medieval Jewish texts and served as Mendelssohn's mentor in Jewish philosophy; he immersed himself in the study of *The Guide for the Perplexed*, which had been recently reprinted under the initiative of none other than his rabbi David Fränkel (the intensive reading of this philosophical work during his earlier youth purportedly caused Mendelssohn's legendary hunchback); he became fluent in German and other European languages, which exposed him to the latest ideas in philosophy and rational religion. He felt especially attracted to natural theology and thirstily imbibed the ideas of Leibniz, Wolff, Locke and others.

FIGURE 16
Portrait of Moses Mendelssohn. His legendary hunchback was attributed to his deep study of Maimonides's philosophical work *The Guide for the Perplexed*.

His friendship with Aaron Solomon Gumperz (1723–1769), one of the Jewish early maskilim he met in Berlin, proved crucial. A university-trained physician and a man of science with intellectual aspirations, Gumperz was well connected to the *Aufklärung* (German Enlightenment) circles in Berlin. He was probably the first Jew to attend the meetings of learned societies devoted to science and philosophy, and even served as secretary to the Royal Academy of Sciences in Berlin, thus becoming closely associated with prominent intellectuals. It was Gumperz who paved Mendelssohn's way into these circles, where the aspiring young intellectual gained immediate recognition and associated with non-Jewish scholars who appreciated the gifted student.

Most prominent among these new friendships was Mendelssohn's acquaintance with Gotthold Ephraim Lessing, the famous German dramatist and preacher of tolerance, who lived in Berlin in the 1750s. Before meeting Mendelssohn, Lessing, probably having Gumperz in mind, had written a one-act comedy titled *Die Juden*, where he introduced a member of this religion as the hero of the story, portrayed in an anti-stereotypical way: as a noble, cultured, charitable man, rather than the unethical, uncultured Jew usually depicted on stage. Lessing's purpose was to point at the possibility – inconceivable for most of his contemporaries – that such a virtuous Jew could exist. In Mendelssohn he found living proof to his assertion. In later years Lessing would write *Nathan der Weise* (Nathan the Wise) (1779), a play advocating religious tolerance, this time modelling his Jewish hero after his new friend. Mendelssohn also became a close confidant and intellectual partner of the author and publisher Friedrich Nicolai, a prominent figure in the German Enlightenment, and throughout the years both collaborated on important literary projects.

FIGURES 17 & 18
Gotthold Ephraim
Lessing and family
(*above*) and Friedrich
Nicolai (*below*), two
of Mendelssohn's
closest friends and
collaborators among
the German *Aufklärer*.

The friendship with these prominent intellectuals opened the doors to the enlightened society, where Mendelssohn gained widespread recognition – occupying in fact an exceptional position for a Jew at the time. Not only was he able to expand his social relationships with German scholars and artists and participate in lively discussions in societies he attended, but he also contributed to the public sphere in a more tangible way through

his writings, publishing at first essays in leading journals and later his own books. Mendelssohn thus became the first Jew to penetrate successfully the republic of letters of the German Enlightenment as a fully fledged member.

A Jewish philosopher of the Aufklärung

None of the early maskilim had come anywhere close to attaining the exceptional position that Mendelssohn would soon occupy in the non-Jewish world as a philosopher of the *Aufklärung*.

Mendelssohn's intellectual activity reached one of its climaxes in 1763, when he successfully participated in the prestigious competition of the Berlin Academy of Sciences – an event that attracted leading thinkers of the time. His *Abhandlung über die Evidenz in Metaphysischen Wissenschaften* (Treatise on Evidence in Metaphysical Sciences) of 1763, the essay he submitted in

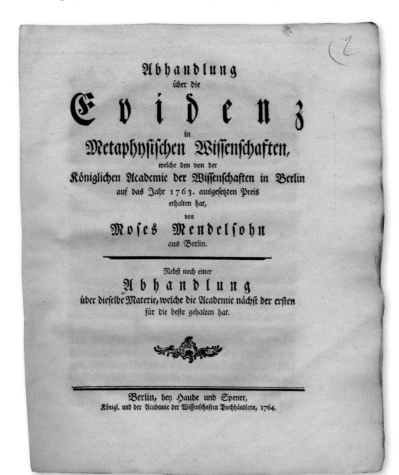

FIGURE 19
Mendelssohn's winning essay at the Berlin Academy of Sciences' contest.

FIGURES 20 & 21 Kant's (*left*) and Mendelssohn's (*right*) essays responding to the question 'What is Enlightenment?', published in the *Berlinische Monatsschrift* in 1784. In the first paragraph of his essay Kant writes: '*Sapere aude!* "Have courage to use your own reason!" – that is the motto of enlightenment.'

response to the question of that year's competition, was awarded the first prize, incidentally surpassing Immanuel Kant, who had also entered the contest. Interestingly, both philosophers would meet again some two decades later, when responding to the famous question posed by the *Berlinische Monatsschrift* (Berlin Monthly), the leading periodical of the Berlin Enlightenment: 'Was ist Aufklärung?' (What is Enlightenment?).

These extraordinary achievements notwithstanding, the work that gained him worldwide celebrity was without doubt *Phaedon oder über die Unsterblichkeit der Seele* (Phaedo or On the Immortality of the Soul). This book, an adaptation of Plato's dialogue *Phaedo* presenting Socrates before his death, reflected Mendelssohn's admiration for Greek philosophers in general and for Socrates in particular. In Mendelssohn's *Phaedon*, Socrates is recast as a modern philosopher, whom Mendelssohn uses as his mouthpiece to defend natural religion and especially one of its central tenets, the belief in the immortality of the soul, which Mendelssohn does relying solely on reason and not on revelation.

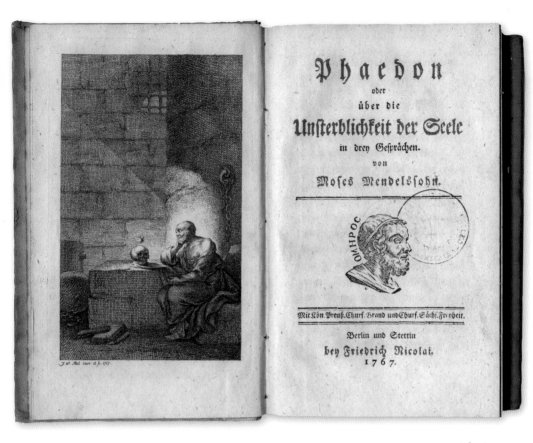

FIGURE 22 (*above*) Mendelssohn's most famous philosophical work, *Phaedon*, with an image of Socrates before his death.

FIGURES 23 & 24 *Phaedon* in Hebrew (*Fedon: hu sefer hash'arat ha-nefesh*) and Italian (*Fedone: O dell' immortalità dell' anima*) translations.

The book was a bestseller: the first edition published in Berlin in 1767 by Friedrich Nicolai was followed by many more – a total of eleven during Mendelssohn's lifetime – and was soon translated into several European languages. Twenty years after its first publication it was rendered into Hebrew by a Jew from Metz, Isaiah Beer-Bing, one of the few maskilim who were active in France.

Mendelssohn and the renewal of Jewish culture

Mendelssohn thus clearly went beyond the confines of the Jewish sphere, within which early maskilim had operated, and entered the European republic of letters, finally achieving a most respectable position therein – if also a contested one, as we

FIGURE 25
Third edition of
Mendelssohn's
commentary to *Be'ur
milot ha-higayon*
from 1784 (first
published in 1761):
Maimonides's
medieval tractate was
updated and edited to
serve modern needs.

shall see. Parallel to his activity in German philosophical circles and not disconnected from it, he also worked hard to cultivate enlightenment among his fellow Jews, embracing goals similar to those of the early maskilim discussed above. Like them, he felt uncomfortable with the restricted range of interest of the Ashkenazi cultural world; he too was distressed with what he saw as Jewish backwardness in the realms of philosophy and science. Joining the initiatives of the early maskilim, who had embarked upon reprinting medieval philosophical works and editing them by inserting their own commentaries and correcting outdated concepts based on eighteenth-century knowledge and philosophy, Mendelssohn sought to contribute to widening the intellectual horizons of the Jews by publishing works that introduced philosophical thought to a Jewish public. It is not surprising that one

FIGURE 26
Shlomo Dubno, Mendelssohn's first partner in the *Be'ur* project.

FIGURE 27
Or li-netivah, the introduction to Mendelssohn's Pentateuch translation and commentary.

of the first and most influential works Mendelssohn published in the field of the Jewish Enlightenment was Maimonides's *Be'ur milot ha-higayon* (Commentary on Logical Terms), a new edition of the twelfth-century logic treatise written by the medieval philosopher that had not been printed since its 1567 Venice edition. Providing his own Hebrew introduction and commentary, Mendelssohn tried to redeem Maimonides's legacy by making it part of the study programme of Jewish scholars, and in fact to turn it into a primer for those taking their first steps in the study of philosophy. As many of his predecessors had done, Mendelssohn employed rhetorical means to make this field of knowledge acceptable, explaining to potential readers that the study of logic was a pursuit necessary to correct

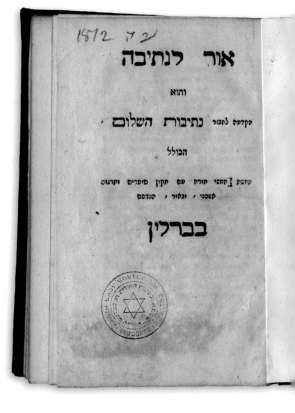

אור לנתיבה

והוא

הקדמה לחבור נתיבות השלום ,

הכולל

תרגום חמשה חומשי תורה עם תקון סופרים ותרגום
לאשכנז , וביאור , הנדפס

בברלין

mistaken beliefs, an instrument that would help people to walk in the paths of righteousness.

However, Mendelssohn's major contribution to the Jewish Enlightenment was undoubtedly *Sefer netivot ha-shalom* (Book of the Paths of Peace), a new edition of the Pentateuch with a High German translation in Hebrew script and a Hebrew commentary. Although this was a collective literary project – he collaborated first with Shlomo Dubno, a Polish maskil and an outstanding scholar of the Hebrew language who tutored Mendelssohn's son, and later enlisted a number of maskilim to write commentaries for the various books – it was mainly Mendelssohn's initiative and his impulse which made it a reality.

FIGURE 28
Mendelssohn's
German translation of
the Book of Psalms.

The *Be'ur* (Commentary), as this project became known, embodied many of the aspirations, the methods and the ideals that came to be identified with the Haskalah, as it crystallized in the later part of the eighteenth century. In *Or li-netivah* (A Light for the Path) (the introduction, which was first published separately from the *Be'ur*) Mendelssohn stressed the importance of making the Bible the chief object of study, rather than the Talmud, which was the authoritative text of Jewish tradition. By translating the Bible into High German, Mendelssohn saw the *Be'ur* as an Enlightenment project and was confident it would become the 'first step to culture' for the Jewish nation.

Considered as an ideal instrument to disseminate maskilic ideas and values, the model of the *Be'ur* was applied by Mendelssohn and by later maskilim to other books of the Bible. Mendelssohn's German translation of the Psalms, which enjoyed great popularity among the German public, was printed in Hebrew script by a later maskil, Joel

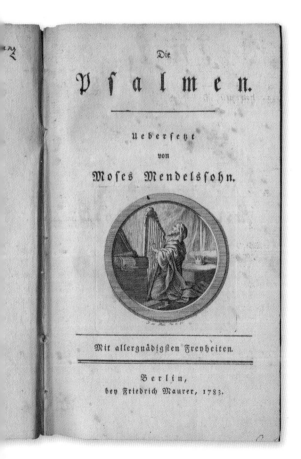

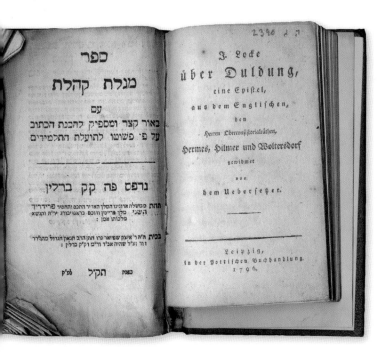

FIGURE 29 (*left*)
Mendelssohn's edition of
Kohelet, published 'for the
benefit of the students', as
the title page reads.

FIGURE 30 (*below*)
First page of
Mendelssohn's *Kohelet*. As
is usual in maskilic texts
introducing scientific and
philosophical concepts,
the new terminology
is rendered in German
translation (in Hebrew
characters). In this first
page of the text, the
Hebrew word *kohelet* is
translated as *der Sammler*
(the collector) or *der
Prediger* (the preacher);
hevel as *Eitelkeit* (vanity),
and so forth.

Brill, in 1785–90, with commentaries appended. A commentary on *Kohelet* (Ecclesiastes), one of the wisdom books of the Bible, had been published by Mendelssohn in 1770 and would appear in a new edition with a German translation of the biblical text soon after his death.

As his most ambitious enterprise in the framework of the Jewish Enlightenment, the *Be'ur* project earned Mendelssohn as much effusive praise as it did threats and condemnation. European Jews who sympathized with the Haskalah expressed their support for its endeavours by subscribing in significant numbers to the *Be'ur*. Among the rabbinical elite, on the other hand, this innovative edition of the Bible provoked diverse reactions. Hirschel Levin (1720–1800), rabbi at Berlin and a close friend of Mendelssohn, provided the work with a formal approbation. Ezekiel Landau (1713–1793), a prominent rabbinical authority from Prague, expressed strong apprehension about the work, while the Chief Rabbi of Altona, Raphael Cohen (1722–1803), harshly opposed it and would have pronounced a ban had he not been prevented from doing so by Danish official intervention. In coming generations the *Be'ur* would move eastward and penetrate traditional circles as a legitimate and often controversial text.

CHAPTER 4

Religious tolerance:
an enlightenment value contested

The lack of tolerance Mendelssohn encountered at the hands of a few traditionalists when he published the *Be'ur* paled in comparison to the intolerance exhibited by certain Christian intellectuals, who confronted him with older calls for conversion, undermining the principle of tolerance which was central to the Enlightenment and which Mendelssohn held so dear.

Throughout his career, Mendelssohn tried to avoid public disputes on theological matters, focusing his discussions on natural religion – that is, the common elements of the different religious beliefs, purportedly derived from reason – rather than on a particular one. But in 1769 Johann Caspar Lavater (1741–1801), a Swiss pastor, forced him to defend publicly his religious beliefs. As a young ministerial candidate temporarily living in Berlin in 1763–64, Lavater had established a friendship with Mendelssohn, and like many admirers paid him several visits. A positive remark regarding Jesus' moral stature made by Mendelssohn during a friendly conversation with Lavater, a Christian millenarian, led the latter mistakenly to assume that the famous Jewish philosopher was ready for conversion; a step he hoped would give rise to a wave of conversion among the Jews. Lavater still recalled Mendelssohn's words when he sent the illustrious philosopher a copy of a religious-philosophical work by Charles Bonnet he had just translated into German. To his translation he had appended a dedicatory epistle addressed to Mendelssohn where, mentioning their fateful conversation, he confronted his Jewish friend with a theological ultimatum, compelling him to refute Bonnet's persuasive proofs of the truth of Christianity or else to accept their validity and convert.

Mendelssohn felt deeply offended by this act, which he saw as a betrayal on the part of Lavater: not only had he dared publish the words he had said about Jesus, casually in a private conversation; he was also jeopardising the very principle that had served as the foundation for their friendship (and, in fact, for Mendelssohn's friendship with other Christian intellectuals) – the principle of religious tolerance, the mutual respect for each other's religious beliefs. Despite his long-standing reticence towards turning his Jewishness into a public issue and exposing his personal views on revealed religion, the great public interest Lavater's ultimatum raised left Mendelssohn almost no choice but to address the challenge openly. His reply, however, did not comply with Lavater's expectations. Instead of defending himself for remaining a Jew, as Lavater had wished, Mendelssohn attacked him for trying to drag him into a religious controversy, a despicable act contravening the values of enlightened culture which both purportedly endorsed. Mendelssohn also employed his 1770 open letter to Lavater, *Schreiben an den Herrn Diaconus Lavater zu Zürich* (Letter to Deacon Lavater at Zurich), to present Judaism as a religion more tolerant than Christianity: whereas Christianity clearly entertained missionary goals, Judaism had no pretension of converting anyone who was not born a Jew, nor claiming it was the sole valid religion (as attested to by the fact that even those who did not abide by the biblical commandments but kept basic moral imperatives – the seven Noahide laws – could aspire to redemption).

Mendelssohn's letter to Lavater elicited a public controversy that did not easily recede from the public agenda. 'The Lavater affair', as this dispute came to be known, generated a significant volume of pamphlets, essays and letters written by leading figures in the German-speaking world willing to express their own opinion regarding the issues at stake. The tension between the two protagonists calmed down after Lavater apologized for his impertinence in a reply to Mendelssohn's letter, *Antwort an Herrn Moses Mendelssohn zu Berlin* (Reply to Mr Moses Mendelssohn in Berlin), issued shortly after the publication of Mendelssohn's text. In a postscript (*Nacherinnerung*) appended to Lavater's reply, Mendelssohn, ignoring the proselytising dreams that the

FIGURE 31 (*opposite*) Mendelssohn and Lavater amicably playing chess, while Lessing watches over them and Fromet, Mendelssohn's wife, acts as an attentive hostess. *Lavater and Lessing with Moses Mendelssohn* (1771?). Painting, 1856, by Moritz Daniel Oppenheim (1800–1882).

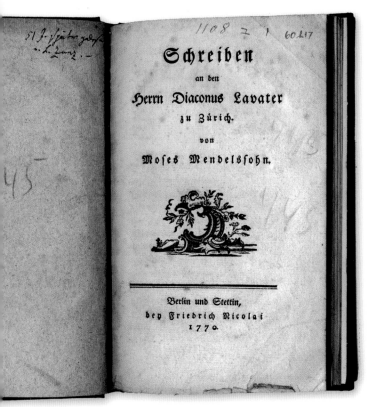

FIGURE 32 Mendelssohn's famous letter to Lavater. 'Mose hat uns das Gesetz geboten, es ist ein Erbtheil der Gemeine Jacob. Alle ubrigen Volker der Erde, glauben wir, seyen von Gott angewiesen worden, sich an das Gesetz der Natur und an die Religion der Patriarchen zu halten. Die ihren Lebeswandel nach den Gesetzen dieser Religion der Natur und der Vernunft einrichten, werden tugendhafte Manner von andern Nationen genennet, und diese sind Kinder der ewigen Seligkeit.'

FIGURE 33 Lavater's reply to Mendelssohn's letter, with a postscript by the latter.

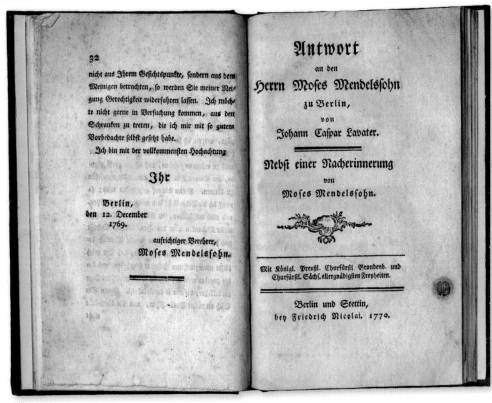

Swiss theologian articulated even more clearly than before in his second missive (by openly stating that it was his wish to see the Jewish philosopher baptized), asked him to put an end to the public confrontation. The affair, however, left a lasting mark and shattered the idea nurtured by Mendelssohn's experience that interfaith relationships were possible.

Tolerance, religion and civil rights

The issue of religious tolerance was not merely a matter of philosophical contemplation or a personal concern for Jewish intellectuals like Mendelssohn and other maskilim who were interested in participating in German intellectual culture. It also served to support claims for ameliorating the legal status of the Jewish minority, and as such it had far-reaching practical implications. During Moses Mendelssohn's time many began to voice the idea of religious tolerance, along with the mercantilist, utilitarian outlook adopted by the state, which called for integrating the Jews, who had been living in German lands as a corporate minority, eradicating discrimination against them as one of the prejudices that prevailed dating from the dark era of religious fanaticism. These ideas fostered by certain German intellectuals and statesmen were heartily embraced by the Jewish mercantile elite and became a central concern of the maskilim.

Both non-Jews and Jews vigorously engaged in the debate surrounding Jewish emancipation. A glimpse at Mendelssohn's interventions in the struggle for emancipation and in the discourse of religious tolerance shows to what extent a Jew of his stature had become an actual partner in this political debate and to what extent this debate developed in a dialogical way, as an exchange between enlightened Jews – at this point represented by Mendelssohn – and German statesmen and men of letters. One of Mendelssohn's most important contributions to the Jewish question was his 1782 preface to the German translation of *Vindiciae Judaeorum* (Vindication of the Jews), a seventeenth-century defence of the Jews' right to return to England written by Manasseh ben Israel, a leading Portuguese Jew in Amsterdam. The *Vindication*, with its refutation of old claims and

prejudices against the acceptance of Jews in society, was seen by Mendelssohn as a worthy contribution to the struggle for Jewish rights. Taking on his predecessor's role as spokesman for the Jews, he decided to acquaint the German public with this apologetic text, and attached a preface to the translation in which he presented his own vision of the future existence of Jews in a tolerant state. The timing was not coincidental: Mendelssohn was in fact explicitly responding to a text that placed the subject of Jewish emancipation at the centre of attention, published the previous year by Christian Wilhelm Dohm (1751–1820): *Ueber die bürgerliche Verbesserung der Juden* (On the Civil Improvement of the Jews).

Dohm's historic treatise, originally printed in 1781 (the new edition that appeared soon afterward, in 1783, is presented here), originated in an appeal that Mendelssohn had received from a distinguished Alsatian Jew, Herz Cerfberr, who requested the famous Jewish philosopher to intercede in favour of Alsatian Jewry by formulating an apologetic tract to be submitted to the

FIGURE 34
Dohm's proposal
for ameliorating
the status of the
Jews in Prussia,
*Ueber die bürgerliche
Verbesserung der
Juden*, a text that
set the tone for the
debate about Jewish
emancipation in
German lands.

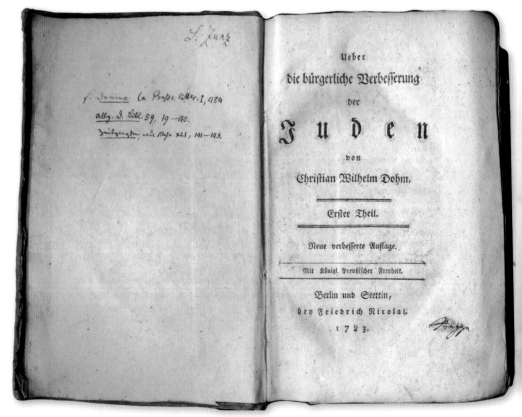

Council of State. Mendelssohn, assuming it would be better if a Christian rather than a Jew pleaded for Jewish rights, suggested Dohm for the task. Dohm was a historian and a high official in the Prussian government who belonged to the enlightened circles of Berlin and had friendly relations with Mendelssohn; since he intended in any case to write a history of the Jews, he readily agreed. After writing the memorandum commissioned by the Alsace Jewish community, Dohm worked on a more extensive treatise on the legal status of the Jews, finally publishing what would become a pivotal text in the discussion of Jewish emancipation.

Dohm argued that Jews should be seen as human beings and not simply as members of a religion. As a humanist and a rationalist, he considered the limitations placed upon the Jews by the Christian state and the inferior status assigned to them on the periphery of society as an unacceptable anomaly, which in fact had led to the lamentable situation of the Jews at that time. Dohm proposed a detailed plan for integrating the Jews into the state, by granting them political rights and promoting a state-supported transformation of the Jews that would rid them of their purported moral corruption and unproductive way of life, for which not their faith but their historical oppression was responsible, and that would reshape them into useful and loyal citizens.

Mendelssohn had been involved in the formulation of Dohm's revolutionary text and he agreed with many of the views put forth by the Prussian bureaucrat, such as his advocacy of civil equality for the Jews and religious tolerance on the part of the state. However, Mendelssohn had serious concerns over Dohm's plan for integrating the Jews into the state. He formulated them in his preamble to *Rettung der Juden*, the German translation of *Vindication of the Jews*. In his tract, Dohm had presented the granting of rights to the Jews as conditional upon their regeneration and productivization. He had spoken of the rehabilitation of the Jews, largely through European education, and of their productivization by redirecting them from commerce to more productive occupations such as agriculture and crafts. Although Mendelssohn agreed in principle with the need

Manasseh Ben Israel

Rettung der Juden

Aus dem Englischen übersetzt.

Nebst einer Vorrede
von
Moses Mendelsfohn.

Als ein Anhang
zu des
Hrn. Kriegsraths Dohm
Abhandlung:
Ueber
die bürgerliche Verbesserung

der Juden.

Mit Königl. Preußischer allergnädigster Freyheit.

Berlin und Stettin
bey Friedrich Nicolai.
1782.

FIGURE 35
The German
translation of
Manasseh ben
Israel's *Vindication
of the Jews*, with
Mendelssohn's
remarkable preface, in
which he first openly
addressed the issue of
the emancipation of
the Jews.

for inner reform among the Jews, he utterly disagreed with turning this into a precondition for the amelioration of Jewish civil status and supported instead the approach that favoured the granting of rights irrespective of any prior internal reform. If Jews are to be integrated into society and culture, he claimed, they must first be liberated from restraints and discrimination; if they are expected to use their hands, let them first be set free.

Furthermore, Mendelssohn disagreed with Dohm, who still favoured the age-old autonomy of the Jewish community. Mendelssohn opposed such a situation as it contradicted the liberal political theory Dohm promoted. More importantly, Mendelssohn fiercely opposed the idea of leaving in the hands of rabbinic authorities the power of excommunication, denying as he did the use of external coercion in private issues of religious and personal beliefs, and considering this a hindrance to a tolerant society. Not least was it perceived by him as a personal danger, as rumours about the threat of a ban against him on account of his *Be'ur* reached him, originating from various Jewish communities.

Mendelssohn's rejection of the ban in his preface to the *Vindication* fuelled a wild controversy, which would confront him again with a call for conversion and would force him to present explicitly his views on religion and Enlightenment. The challenge came this time in the form of an anonymous pamphlet, *Das Forschen nach Licht und Recht in einem Schreiben an Herrn Moses Mendelssohn* (The Search for Light and Right in an Epistle to Moses Mendelssohn), written in 1782 by August Cranz, a member of the German enlightened circles and in fact a defender

of Jewish rights and an ardent admirer of the Jewish philosopher. Cranz, who unlike Lavater was not a clergyman but embraced the same proselytizing goal, used Mendelssohn's disapproval of the rabbinic power of excommunication to call publicly into question his Jewish faith, thus compelling him once again to expose his religious views; only this time Mendelssohn was being forced to choose not between Judaism and Christianity, as in the Lavater affair, but between Judaism and Enlightenment. Cranz, an anticlerical deist who opposed religious fanaticism of any kind, questioned the compatibility between Judaism and Enlightenment, and, more specifically, between rabbinic Judaism and religious tolerance. Mendelssohn was left no choice but to demonstrate that what he had attempted to incarnate all his life, being a loyal Jew and a committed enlightener at one and the same time, was a feasible option and should be vindicated.

Mendelssohn's reply to Cranz's provocative pamphlet, entitled *Jerusalem oder über religiöse Macht und Judenthum* (Jerusalem or On Religious Power and Judaism), published in 1783, became his most important and influential work. In it he affirmed his own unreserved attachment to the Jewish religion and restated his commitment to Mosaic Law, in light of Cranz's assertions as to his weakened faith. Beyond this personal statement, Mendelssohn, aware of the position of leader and spokesman of the Jews he had been forced into, envisioned a more encompassing goal: to present a detailed exposition of Judaism in accordance with rational beliefs, and concomitantly to foster the idea that Jews could and should be integrated into the state as Jews, without being asked to give up their religion or their commandments. Mendelssohn argued that religion was not a matter of coercion but a voluntary

FIGURE 36
Das Forschen nach Licht und Recht, published anonymously in 1782, was the trigger for Mendelssohn's *Jerusalem*, his most famous work on Judaism.

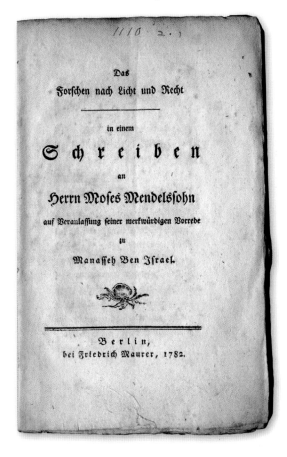

Das

Forschen nach Licht und Recht

in einem

S ch r e i b e n

an

Herrn Moses Mendelssohn

auf Veranlassung seiner merkwürdigen Vorrede

zu

Manasseh Ben Israel.

B e r l i n,
bei Friedrich Maurer, 1782.

Moses Mendelssohns

Morgenstunden

oder

Vorlesungen

über das Daseyn Gottes.

Erster Theil.

Frankfurt und Leipzig,
1786.

FIGURE 37
Morgenstunden,
Mendelssohn's last
philosophical work,
was first published
in 1785 and appeared
in a second, enlarged
edition in 1786.

choice; he explained why no ecclesiastical authority should be
granted coercive power. Furthermore, he insisted that Judaism
in no way contradicted Enlightenment but could rather coexist
with it. He stressed the universal and rational principles in the
Jewish faith, including the existence of God and the immortality
of the soul, and presented Judaism as the faith closest to natural
religion. By thus emphasizing the elements of Jewish religion
that were common to the members of all monotheistic faiths,
he affirmed that the Jewish faith represented no obstacle in the
path of those Jews who wished to enter German and European
society. *Jerusalem* was intended to promote true tolerance and a
pluralistic society, but it was written out of despair and frustration. The optimistic belief of living in a tolerant society, which
was clearly present in the preface to *Vindication of the Jews,*

published only shortly before, had by then patently disappeared and given way to scepticism and suspicion.

Jerusalem was published just three years before Mendelssohn's early passing. But his controversy with Cranz was not his last debate. Mendelssohn was forced to defend the legacy of his dear friend Lessing in *Morgenstunden, oder Vorlesungen über das Daseyn Gottes* (Morning Hours, or Lectures about God's Existence), first published in 1785, shortly before his death in January 1786. Lessing, who had passed away in 1781, was being accused of pantheism, the belief that identifies God with the universe, spread by the Jewish philosopher Baruch Spinoza (1632–1677), which in those days equated to atheism – a terrible accusation in Mendelssohn's eyes. The attack, launched by proponents of a rising stream of counter-Enlightenment, was in fact directed against the rational theology that Lessing and Mendelssohn had always endorsed. Mendelssohn felt obliged to take upon himself, for what would be the last time in his life, a defence of the philosophical and religious rationalism of the Enlightenment.

Mendelssohn's passing at the early age of 56 put an abrupt end to his active participation in philosophical, theological and political controversies, but his writings and his image continued to play a decisive role far beyond his time.

CHAPTER 5

A curriculum for Jewish education: rabbinic ideas contested

MENDELSSOHN WAS NOT ALONE in his call for enlightenment and reform in Jewish life. From the 1780s onwards other maskilim were developing coherent ideologies calling for the transformation of Jewish society. One of the most influential texts of the Haskalah was *Divre shalom ve-emet* (Words of Peace and Truth), written by Mendelssohn's friend and collaborator the Hebrew poet, linguist and biblical scholar Hartwig (Naphtali Herz) Wessely. This slim pamphlet, published in Berlin in 1782, caused a great stir in the Jewish world, perhaps more than any other single maskilic text in the eighteenth century. It inspired the supporters of the Haskalah, but at the same time provoked a controversy that would agitate the Jewish world and would induce its author to adopt a defensive position in three additional 'epistles' he appended, the last of which, *Rehovot* (Paths) is presented here.

Wessely wrote his pamphlet in response to the Edict of Toleration issued by the Austrian Emperor Joseph II in 1781 – that is, shortly after the publication of Dohm's advocacy of Jewish emancipation. Although the Emperor's regulations introduced almost no substantial change in the status of the Jews – neither citizenship nor equal rights were granted, and many of the existing legal restrictions prevailed – they aroused enthusiasm among certain circles in Jewish society, first and foremost the maskilim. They were especially thrilled by the educational reforms promulgated by Joseph II: Jews were compelled to establish German schools in which their children would receive general education and would be instructed in handicrafts and 'productive' occupations; they were also allowed to attend non-Jewish schools. Inspired by this encouraging resolution that

seemed so compatible with maskilic aspirations – but would soon prove disappointing – Wessely published early in 1782 his *Divre shalom ve-emet*, an open letter addressed to the Jews living in Habsburg lands, calling for the implementation of the imperial decree and deploying his vision for a radical change in the content and nature of Jewish education.

In his pamphlet, Wessely outlined the first systematic curriculum for modern Jewish education. His proposed curriculum would from then on guide the pedagogical efforts of the maskilim regarding modern Jewish education – a subject that would figure prominently in subsequent maskilic publications. Wessely developed a distinction between two realms of knowledge: *torat ha-adam*, the 'teaching of man' or 'human knowledge', and *torat ha-Shem*, meaning 'teaching of God' or 'divine knowledge'. Wessely called for a continuation in devoting time to *torat ha-Shem*, that is, to the study of the Bible and the Talmud – but not to the exclusion of *torat ha-adam* (secular studies), as he claimed had been the custom in Ashkenazi society for several centuries. Divine knowledge was superior, he maintained, but in order to understand the depth of it 'human knowledge' was indispensable. Knowledge of history and geography, natural science and mathematics, for instance, was necessary for understanding the Bible and it could corroborate the veracity of the sacred text. The study of the vernacular from a young age was also indispensable, as this helped Jews to understand the meaning of the Hebrew sacred texts. In addition, it helped them achieve a practical goal – economic success in their commercial ventures and in their association with others.

Wessely's reformist programme contained demands which were revolutionary vis-à-vis traditional Jewish education, and, as such, infuriated the traditional elite. They attacked him for legitimizing secular studies by placing secular knowledge before 'divine knowledge', thus demoting the ideal of Talmudic scholarship. It was this subversive plan to transform Jewish education, coupled with the fact that when presenting his plan Wessely had dared to usurp the position of the rabbis by stepping up as an authoritative spokesman of the Jews (though he patently lacked religious authority or a rabbinical position), that elicited the

FIGURE 38
Hartwig (Naphtali Herz) Wessely.

מכתב רביעי

כתוב

גם הוא לאחינו בני ישראל / ה' יגן עליהם · הוא יפרש
דברי המכתב הראשון / ויורה כי אמריו לדקו יחדיו / אין
בהם נפתל ועקש · ויוסיף לדבר עוד בענין סדר הלמוד
וגדול הבנים · ולפי שהקורא בו יתהלך ברחבה · גם עתה
הרחיב ה' לנו על פי עדותן של חכמים וסופרים
המזכרים במכתב השלישי / על כן

קראנו שם המכתב הזה

רחובות

נפתלי הרץ וייזל

ברלין

בדפוס האינסטיטוט חנוך נערים / תחת פקודת יד האדיהם
וחונכיהם כ"ה הנדיבים הקצינ' התורנים כת"ר איצק בן כ"וח הקצין
הנכבד כ"ר דניאל יפה יל"ו / וכה"ר דוד פרידלענדר יל"ו :

Berlin.

Im Verlag der Jüdischen Freyschule

FIGURE 39
Rehovot, the fourth
and last 'epistle' in
the *Divre shalom
ve-emet* series.

anger of the rabbinic elite. In the wake of his epistle, Wessely was harshly attacked by the leading rabbis of the time – prominently Ezekiel Landau in Prague and David Tevele in Lissa in Western Poland – who branded Wessely a heretic and declared him an enemy of Judaism.

Wessely could have never foreseen the polemic caused by his text, and certainly had no intention of causing it. Although he was a man of the eighteenth-century Enlightenment, comfortable in European culture – he was fluent in German, read newspapers and philosophy books, and dressed in modern fashion – he was by no means a freethinker but remained an observant Jew, whose main concern was the Hebrew language. A biographical detail that greatly moulded his stance was his proximity to Sephardic culture. Born in Hamburg and raised in Copenhagen, he had spent formative years in Amsterdam, where he was closely associated with Sephardic intellectual circles, before moving to Berlin. When writing his epistle he was clearly influenced by the kind of education he had seen among Sephardic Jews, whom he admired much – to the point that when living late in life in Hamburg, he asked to be buried after his death in the Portuguese section of the Altona cemetery, as in fact happened.

Astounded by the fierce offensive of the rabbinic elite against him and his pamphlet, Wessely adopted an apologetic position, though without losing his militant tone. In three additional epistles, he defended himself against the accusations raised against him, claiming his intentions had been misunderstood. He clarified his arguments and presented his claims in a milder way, without however retracting his central points. Wessely did not stand alone in fighting this battle. For one thing, he enjoyed the endorsement of the Jewish communities in northern Italy, who needed no inducement to introduce changes. They in fact had already embraced the ideals that Wessely was promoting, and indeed their lifestyle reflected his notions regarding the desirable pattern of Jewish life. Wessely also drew great comfort and full support from maskilic circles in Berlin, who saw his case as a *cause célèbre*. Headed by Mendelssohn – who in those days was publishing his preface to the *Vindication of the*

Jews and was calling on the rabbis to embrace the principle of toleration – the Berliners vigorously defended their close friend against the rabbinical front rising against him. These groups in turn were backed by non-Jewish intellectuals, August Cranz among them. Shortly before printing his provocative pamphlet defying Mendelssohn to defend his faith, Cranz intervened in the polemic surrounding Wessely's pamphlet. Using Enlightenment rhetoric, Cranz addressed Prince Sulkowsky of Lissa, informed him of the attack being launched on Wessely from his city by Rabbi Tevele of Lissa, and, presenting the rabbi's behaviour as religious persecution motivated by a fanatic drive, was able to secure the Polish prince's support for the maskilic front.

Hartwig Wessely represented a new type of Jewish intellectual: one who did not lose his commitment to faith, the study of Torah and the observance of the Commandments, but, on the other hand, no longer belonged to the circle of Talmudic scholars. This maskilic intellectual, whose interests lie in the fields of literature, poetry, and linguistic and biblical studies, was no longer defined by his Talmudic scholarship or his rabbinic and community role, but rather by his ideas and intellectual capacity. He drew his authority and ideas from his new reading of all aspects of Jewish tradition, from his analysis of reality and his rational judgement. Emerging from within the traditional society, Wessely and the other members of the new elite gradually broke away from the rabbinical elite, which until then had enjoyed total exclusivity in the world of the book, knowledge, and the spiritual guidance of the Jews, and established an autonomous movement that eventually engendered a profound transformation of Jewish society and culture.

CHAPTER 6

The Haskalah movement:
its ideology and institutions

IT WAS ONLY in the 1780s that the Haskalah became an organized movement, with its own institutions, means of communication and, most importantly, detailed programme to bring about immediate changes in Jewish society according to a well-defined ideology. Before that the maskilim had either worked independently or cooperated ad hoc in specific projects. The organizational setting that was then introduced followed patterns of organization and activity that prevailed in the European Enlightenment.

The movement was born out of maskilic societies, the first of which was founded by a group of young and ambitious intellectuals in Königsberg in Eastern Prussia that included scholars proficient in the religious sources, students knowledgeable in the sciences and in Greek and Latin literature, and sons of upper-class families attracted to the world of books. Imitating the hundreds of reading and literary societies that emerged in German cities in the eighteenth century, in particular in its last two decades, the members of this group created at the end of 1782 the Hevrat Dorshe Leshon Ever (Society of Friends of the Hebrew Language), a voluntary association that provided a social and cultural framework promoting maskilic goals and values. A branch was soon established in Berlin, and new maskilic associations with similar interests would start appearing in other German cities. Voluntary societies were not an exceptional feature of Jewish life in the eighteenth century. What was unique about these maskilic associations was the fact that, rather than being 'holy societies', devoted to religious or community purposes, these were secular ones – in nature, in the wording of their statutes and in their objectives – the paramount aim of their

ה מ א ס ף
ל ש נ ת
ה ת ק מ ו
כולל שירים ומכתבים
אשר נאספו ונקבצו יחד על ידי אנשי
חברת דורשי לשון עבר
בקענינגסב׳ערג׃

קעניגסבערג שנת תק׳מ׳ו
נדפס בבית החדפים דניאל קרישטאף קאנטר
בדפוסו ונחתיות החברה ׃

FIGURE 40
Title page of
ha-Me'asef. This first
Hebrew periodical
was published in
Königsberg and later
in Berlin.

activity being to disseminate enlightenment and the light of reason among its
members, and lead a cultural revolution
in the Jewish world.

As a society whose declared mission
was to convey its maskilic message to
the Jewish masses and mobilize public
opinion, it is not surprising that one of
the first and immediate endeavours of
the Society of Friends of the Hebrew
Language was to set up a means of
communication in the fashion of the
periodicals and journals that were so
popular in Europe in the eighteenth
century. In 1783 they began publishing
ha-Me'asef (in German Der Sammler,
The Gatherer). This Hebrew–German
periodical was widely distributed among
subscribers in numerous cities, both in
Germany and beyond (for instance in
Amsterdam, Copenhagen, Strasbourg
and Vilnius). Attempting to engender
a transformation of Jewish society and
culture, the innovative journal included
a wide range of sections that exposed its
readers to various fields of knowledge and science, provided
information and reviews on new books that were relevant to
the maskilic discourse, and published original and translated
Hebrew poetry. As the forerunner of a modern newspaper, ha-
Me'asef contained a news section, which reported on historical
changes and events, especially pertaining to the Jews in various
communities. It also printed commentaries on biblical verses,
clarifications on Hebrew grammar and historical biographies of
famous Jews, but also, for instance, a patriotic entry on the life
of Frederick the Great following his death.

The journal aimed not only to present the ideas and opinions
of the members of the society and the fruit of their literary
endeavours to a large readership; it also envisioned a broader

FIGURE 41 (*above*)
This illustration of
a diver appeared
in a piece written
by Baruch Lindau
(1759–1849) that
would later be
included in his *Reshit
Limudim* (Beginning
of Learning), the
most popular and
updated scientific
Hebrew textbook
at the end of the
eighteenth century.

FIGURE 42 (*left*)
A Hebrew eulogy
in memory of Moses
Mendelssohn,
published in *ha-
Me'asef* shortly after
his death.

FIGURE 43 (*right*)
A biographical note on Frederick II, king of Prussia, published in one of the 1786 *ha-Me'asef* issues after the death of the monarch. This text was preceded by a patriotic poem on the occasion of Frederick William II's accession to the throne.

FIGURE 44 (*below*)
Ha-me'asef from 1786, with its German supplement. As indicated on the title page, this periodical was published by the Society of Friends of the Hebrew Language, under the supervision of Isaac Euchel.

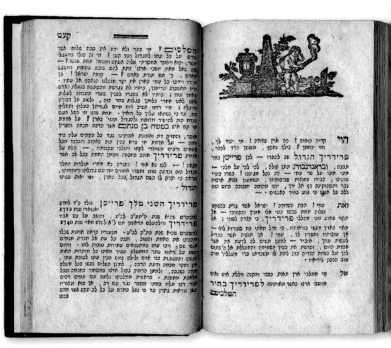

objective – to establish a Jewish literary community that would extend beyond geographical boundaries and connect Jews from distant places, living far beyond the limits of Königsberg and even Prussia. *Ha-Me'asef* encouraged an ongoing dialogue between the journal and its readership by inviting readers to write letters and to answer questions and riddles put forward by the editors. In fact, it served as a forum in which any Jew, religious or lay, could freely present his thoughts and proposals to a broad audience, and as such it fostered the aim of the Haskalah of expanding its circle of activists and supporters.

Although the establishment of the society and the periodical was a cooperative project, the guiding spirit behind these initiatives was Isaac Euchel (1756–1804). Born in Copenhagen to a family of merchants, he had spent several years of his youth in Berlin before moving to Königsberg. There he attended the city's famed university, one of his teachers being the renowned philosopher Immanuel Kant. While in Königsberg, Euchel served as a tutor at the home of the Friedländers, a wealthy family that provided vital support and patronage to the maskilim. As the teacher of Rebecca Friedländer, he developed a close relationship with the young student, to whom he dedicated a work he published in 1786: his *Gebete der Juden*, a translation of the Jewish prayer book into German – this being one of the very rare cases in which a maskil addressed a female public. (Incidentally the same year a maskil from the Friedländer family, David, published in Berlin his own translation of the prayer book into German, though in Hebrew letters, also dedicated to two Jewish women.) Euchel became the first editor of *ha-Me'asef*, and in this role he was able to consolidate the journal, attract a significant number of subscribers, and expand the connections of the society and the periodical with Berlin. In 1787 he moved to the Prussian capital, which by then had already become the leading centre of the Haskalah – to some extent thanks to Euchel's tireless efforts.

The maskilic printing press in Berlin

When Euchel arrived in Berlin, he encountered a thriving maskilic culture. In fact, he had moved to this city having been

FIGURES 45 & 46
In Euchel's edition
(*right*) well-known
hymns are added
for the female users,
which substitute
the *techinnah*, the
Yiddish supplications
composed for women,
of which the author
could not approve. In
Friedländer's edition
(*left*), the German
translation in Hebrew
script of the *Shema
Israel* (Hear oh Israel)
prayer.

called to lead one of the most important maskilic institutions
that had been established there: a printing house specifically
devoted to promoting the alternative Jewish maskilic culture and
disseminating its ideology. This unique publishing house was
created in 1784 in connection with yet another innovative institution, a modern school founded in 1778 by wealthy members
of the Berlin Jewish community. The school was intended for
the children of poor Jews and was called *Hinukh Ne'arim*, or
the *Freyschule* (Free School). A reformative Enlightenment
project par excellence, this school was the first educational
institution in Ashkenazi Jewry to include languages, science
and European culture in its curriculum, as part of its efforts
to prepare Jewish youth as productive and moral citizens. As
a philanthropic institution, the school obtained a licence from
the government to establish a Hebrew printing house to help
finance its activities. The outcome was *Hevrat Hinukh Ne'arim*, in
German the *Orientalische Buchdruckerei* (Oriental Press), which
became instrumental in disseminating the Haskalah.

Though a Hebrew printing press was certainly not a new phenomenon in the Jewish world, the *Orientalische Buchdruckerei* was exceptional in being driven by an ideology meant to serve modern transformative aims, to disseminate knowledge and science, to further the improved education of youth, and to increase the number of readers of Haskalah literature. In its years of activity, especially until the end of the eighteenth century, it enriched the library of the Haskalah with dozens of books and publications.

The printing press being directly connected to the new educational institution, one of its goals was to publish new textbooks for Jewish pupils. The educational reforms preached by the maskilim, and more specifically by Wessely's programme, called for the introduction of new learning contents and also the use of new methods, and this entailed the production of adequate learning materials. The maskilim, many of whom were teachers who adopted modern educational ideals and worked in new Jewish schools, heartily embraced this task and authored a

FIGURE 47
Sefer ha-midot, a book of morals published as part of Wessely's plan to reform Jewish education.

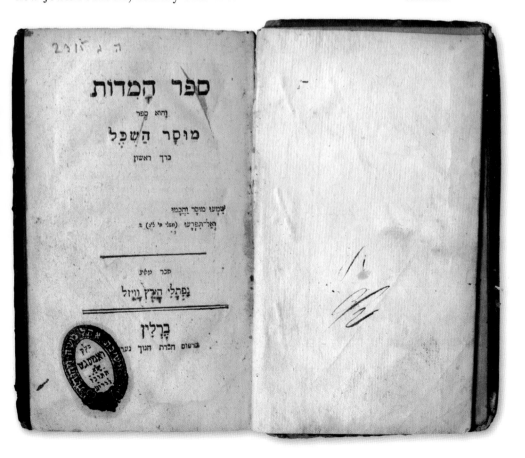

FIGURE 48
Avtalyon, an
innovative 1790
reader based on
the stories of the
Bible. Here depicted
is King Saul, in
vocalized Hebrew
for the benefit of
students learning the
Hebrew language,
accompanied
by grammatical
explanations in
German in Hebrew
script.

staggering number of new textbooks, many of which appeared in print at the *Orientalische Buchdruckerei*. A textbook evincing this new kind of pedagogical orientation was *Sefer ha-midot* (Book of Ethics), an ethical treatise published by Wessely, apparently in 1787. Wessely, like other maskilim, placed special emphasis on the moral rehabilitation of the Jews. As mentioned above, in his *Words of Peace and Truth* he expressed a theoretical model for educational reform; with the *Book of Ethics* he gave an example of his new approach. Directed at youngsters it offered a model for combining a commitment to Torah and *mitzvoth* (commandments) with the obligations of a Jew as a human being and as a citizen of the state.

Pedagogically even more innovative was *Avtalyon* (1790), a reader for the instruction of youngsters, containing Bible stories in simple prose. Its author was Aaron Wolfsohn (1756–1835), a private tutor and one of the most prominent maskilim in

the 1790s (in fact a frequent contributor to *ha-Me'asef* and its future editor). Wolfsohn's work, the first Hebrew non-religious book written specifically for the education of Jewish children, employed contemporary theories on education to stimulate a curiosity that would make students more receptive to its teachings and more active in the learning process. Wolfsohn's book emphasized reason and universal moral lessons culled from the Bible rather than particularistic messages found in rabbinic works. *Avtalyon* became a success: it was reprinted several times in the next three decades, and became a model for later Hebrew textbooks.

The official permit that the *Orientalische Buchdruckerei* received from the Prussian government was limited to printing books in Hebrew (actually in 'oriental languages', hence its name). This stipulation was in accordance with the maskilic desire to renew the Hebrew language and with the belief, present since the efforts of the early maskilim, that Hebrew was a flexible, living language that could be used for any genre or discipline. One of the immediate goals of this printing press was in fact to demonstrate the capability of Hebrew to serve as a modern means of communication, which it tried to show by publishing texts of very different kinds, including poetry, philosophy and ethics, science, pedagogy, and, from 1788 onwards, the periodical *ha-Me'asef*.

In the efforts to revive the Hebrew language and to strengthen Jewish pride, the cooperation between the new intellectual elite and the Jewish economic elite proved indispensable. The maskilim who published works at the *Orientalische Buchdruckerei* often enjoyed the financial support of wealthy Jews from Berlin and other German cities, without whose help their ambitious projects would have been impossible to realize. This support, which had existed since the earliest days of the Haskalah and was still sorely needed even after a maskilic printing house was founded, became crucial, particularly in the case of a protracted enterprise in which Wessely embarked on in the 1780s: the publication of *Shire tif'eret* (Poems of Glory), a biblical epic depicting the life of Moses and the exodus of the Jews from Egypt paraphrasing relevant fragments from the Bible. It was

2626 א ד

Die Moseide

in

achtzehn Gesängen.

Uebersetzt nach dem hebräischen Original

von

Hartwig Wessely,

mit

neuen teutschen Anmerkungen

des Verfassers.

Erstes Heft.

Berlin,
In Kommission bei Wilhelm Vieweg. 1791.

השיר האחד עשר

יְיָ הַצַּדִּיק כִּי מִי כָמֹהוּ
בּוֹרֵא אֶרֶץ חֹשֶׁךְ תֹּהוּ וָבֹהוּ
וּבְצַדְקָתוֹ לִיצוּרָיו הֵכִינָהּ
תַּחַת חֹשֶׁךְ בִּדְבַר פִּיו אוֹר הוֹפִיעַ
תַּחַת בֹּהוּ יָם פָּשָׂה רָקִיעַ
תַּחַת תֹהוּ שָׂם כַּנְחָרֹתָיהָ

א   ‏ ‏

FIGURES 49 & 50
The biblical Hebrew
epic *Shire tif'eret* by
Wessely (*left*), and its
German translation,
Die Moseide (*right*).

only with the support of various patrons who
were sympathetic to the goals of the Haskalah
that the serial publication of this ambitious
project – which started with the release of the
first volume at the maskilic printing press in
Berlin in 1789 – was accomplished. Inspired
perhaps by Klopstock's famous epic *Messiah*,
and probably wishing to show that outstanding
poetical achievement was also feasible in modern-day Hebrew,
this celebrated work became emblematic of the Hebrew literary accomplishments of the Haskalah. Its popularity among
non-Jewish German intellectuals is attested to by its partial
translation, which appeared under the title *Die Moseide*. The
German edition of *Shire tif'eret* was accomplished in part by
two of Wessely's admirers, the German professors Hufnagel and
Spalding, and in cooperation with the author, who provided a
German introduction and his own remarks.

A key figure in the Berlin Haskalah, who served as manager of the *Orientalische Buchdruckerei*, was Isaac Satanow (1732–1796) a compulsive writer and publisher of Hebrew books from Galicia. He used his position to further his own writing projects. One of his earliest works published shortly after he settled in Berlin was *Sefer ha-ḥizayon* (Book of Revelations) (1775), in which he imitates the literary style of the medieval Hebrew poet Alharizi, and shows the splendour of the Hebrew language. In the book he deals also with scientific topics and, interestingly, depicts life on the moon. Besides the publication of original works – many of them presented as ancient manuscripts that had been only recently discovered in private libraries, but were in fact fruit of his own imagination – Satanow ascribed much importance to reprinting books of Jewish thought from the medieval and Renaissance periods, most of which had never been reissued after the sixteenth century. Such was the case of *Mahberot 'Immanu'el* (Immanuel's Compositions), an audacious collection of witty tales in verse composed by the Jewish poet and writer Immanuel of Rome, a contemporary of Dante and a close friend of Italian poets, that had been out of print since its second edition of 1535.

Mahberot 'Immanu'el was unique in the erotic, disconcerting descriptions and seemingly obscene poems it presented. Those such as Wessely had warned younger maskilim for being taken in by such works, yet Satanow regarded it as a model of superb literary writing reflecting the beauty of prose evinced by the Song of Songs. Only after he persuaded Isaac Daniel Itzig (1750–1806), a member of the wealthy Itzig family, one of the founders of the *Freyschule* and the printing house and a champion of the Haskalah, to purchase a rare copy of the first edition was Satanow able to prepare his own new edition of the book.

FIGURE 51
Sefer ha-ḥizayon, an original work by Isaac Satanow, one of the first in a long list of publications.

מחברות
עמנואל

מליץ ומליפר , הנותן אמר שפר , בסיפור וספר , ישא בשיר
קולו , במליצה חידה משלו , בשקל הקודש מהללו , ללמד לבני
יהודה צחות , למליצים שיחות , להשביע לקוראיו שובע שמחות

חברו ראש המדברים , ואבי המשוררים , הכם חרשים
ונבון לחשים , מהו עמנואל , בהר"ר שלמה ז"ל

כי ממתקים , מדברותיו מנופת מתוקים , מין אל זן צחות מפיקים , וזהב המליצה
בעליהם מריקים , הוא גאל המושגות , רוא המשביר צחות לבעלי המליצות ,
ברוח פיו יחיה הדוממים , בשפתו ישיח אלמים , ובמ"דברו ינובב שפלים
ורמים , יקרא אל צבא מרום במרום ויענהו , ואל צבא
האדמה בארמה וישיבוהו ,

יעלה שמים ירד תהומות , יחשוף סתומות , יגלה תעלומות ,
יבין שמועות , יספר נוראות , ועל אל אלים ידבר נפלאות ,

הספר היקר הזה כבר נדפס פעמים בקונסטאנטינא , ועתה אין ממנו אפילו אחד במדינה ,
נייקר פדיון כפשו ונתן בסך עשרים אדומים לקחנה , והנה נדבה רוח איש שר וגדול
ליהודים כניא ח"י ויען למלך פריזין יר"ה ואב."ענט ליסיסי צרפת , פוה
המכם השלם מו' איצק בר"ד יפה להדפיסו ביתר שאת, ויתר עזו ,
פניקול כשירים בהגהה רבה , ובכיחור כנוות וחיכות משקל כל
עיר וייען לקונהו כסן ג' ר"ט ח"ג , ומי חכם יבין
מעלות זה הספר עד אפס ערוך לראשונים חלו ,

ברלין
שנת אזן ׀ וְתִקֵּן ׀ משלים ׀ הרבה ·

Berlin 1796. In der Orientalischen Buchdruckerey.

CHAPTER 7

Jewish intellectuals in the non-Jewish sphere

BY THE TURN of the century Jews were in a very different situation from that at its onset, now on the brink of making a grand entrance into the cultural world of science, literature, philosophy and, shortly afterwards, the arts. In the waning years of the eighteenth century, Jewish physicians were not only striving to disseminate new concepts among their co-religionists as before, but also to contribute to a wider scientific discourse by publishing books and essays for a European public. Jewish philosophers were immersing themselves in the study of new philosophical trends, examining to what extent these trends helped promote a new, appealing interpretation of Judaism, and discussing the latest theoretical fashions in a wider, non-Jewish context through a notable range of publications; Jewish writers were not just experimenting with Hebrew, but were daring to use European languages that until recently they had not really mastered. These Jewish intellectuals had the desire to enter the European republic of letters, an aspiration that may have seemed an unrealistic dream to the early maskilim, but was becoming much more of a reality as the century drew to an end.

A Jewish poet who was able to secure a place for himself in the German literary sphere was Isachar Falkensohn-Behr (1746–1817). Born in Lithuania, he spent time in Berlin, where he frequented early maskilic circles, before moving to Russia, where he practised medicine. Falkensohn-Behr was recognized in German literary circles because of his book *Gedichte von einem pohlnischen Juden* (Poems by a Polish Jew), published anonymously in 1772 and reviewed by Goethe that same year in the *Frankfurter Gelehrten Anzeigen*. This was the first poetry collection published by a Jew in German, an achievement all

the more remarkable considering that its author was not even German-born and had only learnt the language as an adult.

Of a different nature was the literary activity of Moses Wessely (1737–1792), a brother of Hartwig Wessely. A native of Copenhagen, Moses Wessely lived as a merchant in Hamburg, where he maintained a close relationship with leading non-Jewish intellectuals, businessmen, statesmen and princes. Throughout the years, he published essays in German periodicals dealing mainly with banking and commerce, such as the article 'Ueber die Mittel, die Dänischen Staaten gegen Verringerung ihrer Münzen, den Fall ihres Wechselcourses u.s.w. zu sichern' (On the means to insure the Danish states against the devaluation of their coins, the fall of their rate of exchange, etc.). At least one of his contributions, however – a review of Dohm's famous tract – dealt with an issue related to the Jews. Wessely's essays were collected posthumously and published in Berlin in 1798 under the title *Hinterlassene Schriften* (Posthumous Works), the profits being 'for the benefit of his widow', who was left penniless

FIGURE 53
Isachar Falkensohn-Behr's *Gedichte von einem pohlnischen Juden*, the first collection of German poems published by a Jew.

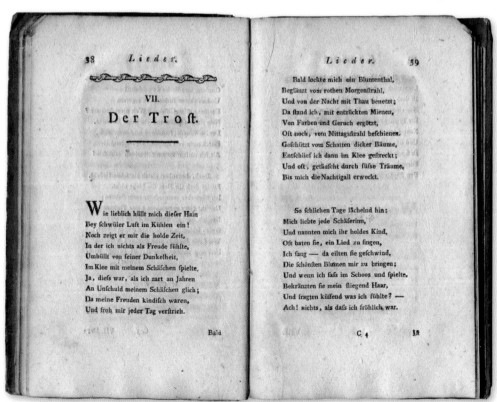

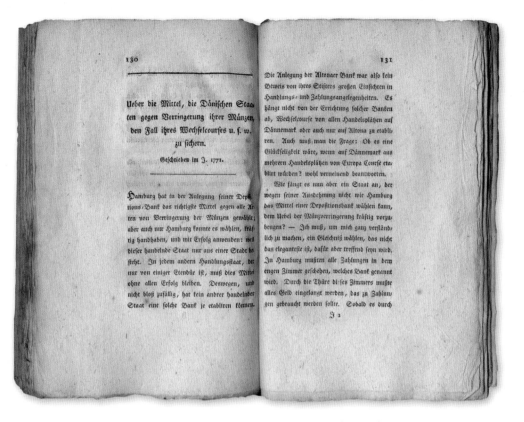

Ueber die Mittel, die Dänischen Staaten gegen Verringerung ihrer Münzen, den Fall ihres Wechselcourses u. ſ. w. zu ſichern.

Geſchrieben im J. 1771.

Hamburg hat in der Anlegung ſeiner Depoſitions-Bank das richtigſte Mittel gegen alle Arten von Verringerung der Münzen gewählt; aber auch nur Hamburg konnte es wählen, kräftig handhaben, und mit Erfolg anwenden: weil dieſer handelnde Staat nur aus einer Stadt beſteht. In jedem andern Handlungsſtaat, der nur von einiger Ebenbüe iſt, muß dies Mittel ohne allen Erfolg bleiben. Deswegen, und nicht bloß zufällig, hat kein andrer handelnder Staat eine ſolche Bank je etabliren können.

Die Anlegung der Altonaer Bank war alſo kein Beweis von ihres Stifters großen Einſichten in Handlungs- und Zahlungsangelegenheiten. Es hängt nicht von der Errichtung ſolcher Banken ab, Wechſelcourſe von allen Handelsplätzen auf Dännemark oder auch nur auf Altona zu etabliren. Auch muß man die Frage: Ob es eine Glückſeligkeit wäre, wenn auf Dännemark aus mehrern Handelsplätzen von Europa Courſe etablirt würden? wohl verneinend beantworten.

Wie fängt es nun aber ein Staat an, der wegen ſeiner Ausdehnung nicht wie Hamburg das Mittel einer Depoſitionsbank wählen kann, dem Uebel der Münzverringerung kräftig vorzubeugen? — Ich muß, um mich ganz verſtändlich zu machen, ein Gleichniß wählen, das nicht das eleganteſte iſt, dafür aber treffend ſeyn wird. In Hamburg mußten alle Zahlungen in dem engen Zimmer geſchehen, welches Bank genannt wird. Durch die Thüre dieſes Zimmers mußte alles Geld eingelangt werden, das zu Zahlungen gebraucht werden ſollte. Sobald es durch

J 2

after Wessely's death in poverty. These texts reflect the self-confidence of this Jewish author, who dared to appear on the public stage as a political economist and express his opinion in a European language for a non-Jewish public, and who considered himself part of the general republic of letters.

An even more impressive intervention into European intellectual life was that made by Marcus Bloch (1723–1799), a leading Jewish physician and scientist in Berlin. Bloch identified with the goals of the Haskalah and supported its major projects; but it was as a man of science acting in the European public sphere that he gained his reputation. As a world expert in the field of ichthyology, Bloch made groundbreaking contributions, publishing a twelve-volume encyclopaedic work that provided a full description of German and foreign fish, with magnificent illustrations. The beginning of this serial publication was received with such enthusiasm in Germany that patronage for publishing future volumes was soon secured. Other works penned by Bloch included a medical treatise on intestinal worms, published

FIGURE 54
The essays published by Moses Wessely in German journals were collected after his death in *Hinterlassene Schriften*.

FIGURE 55 (*above*)
Marcus Bloch, Jewish
physician and famous
ichthyologist.

FIGURE 56 (*below*)
Marcus Herz,
German Jewish
physician and
philosopher.
Mezzotint by Karl
Wilhelm Seeliger
(1766–1821) after
painting by Friedrich
Georg Weitsch
(1758–1828).

originally in German and translated into French as *Traité de la génération des vers des intestins et des vermifuges* (Treatise on the generation of intestinal worms and the means of their extermination), printed in Strasbourg in 1788. This work was submitted in a competition launched by the Copenhagen Royal Academy of Science and received a prize. As the title page of this treatise attests, Bloch was affiliated with leading European scientific societies and had been granted honorary titles that celebrated his extraordinary intellectual achievements.

Another physician who took part in the European Enlightenment, writing not only about science as Bloch had done, but also about metaphysical matters, was Marcus Herz (1747–1803). Herz had studied medicine at the University in Königsberg, where he had been a student of the German philosopher Immanuel Kant, and after completing his studies moved to Berlin. In the Prussian capital he joined maskilic circles and even made a significant contribution to *ha-Me'asef*. He also took part in the bitter controversy between Jewish enlighteners and traditionalists surrounding the issue of early burial. The traditional Jewish custom of burying the dead as early as possible was being strongly attacked by the maskilim as a practice that opposed recent scientific discoveries, which indicated that certainty of death could not be established for at least three days. Herz published, in 1787, an essay in the German section of *ha-Me'asef* under the title *Über die frühe Beerdigung der Juden* (On the early burial of the Jews), subsequently printed in Hebrew and reissued in a second German edition as an independent publication. In this polemical text he defended the scientific position and pleaded for deferring burial, intimidating his adversaries with horrifying stories of cases where people considered dead had been buried too hastily and later revived in their graves.

Herz's support for the activity of the Haskalah notwithstanding, his greatest contribution was to the European Enlightenment. He gained a large measure of social prestige through the lectures he delivered and the scientific experiments he

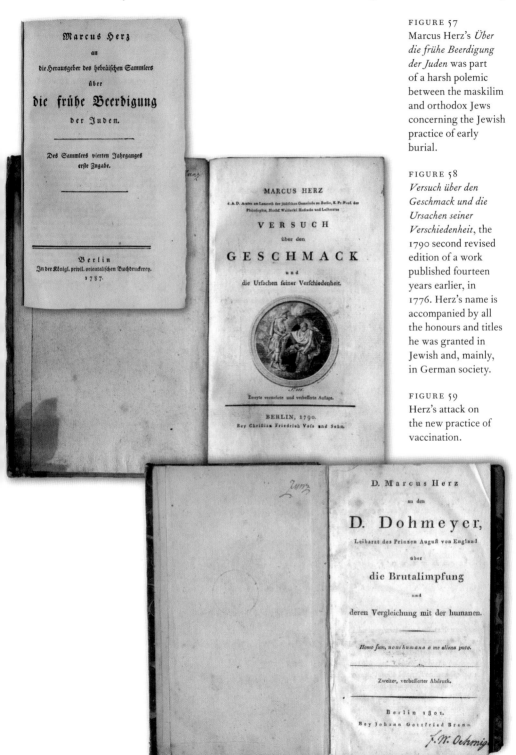

FIGURE 60
Portrait of Salomon
Maimon, painted
in the 1790s.
Distinguishing
Jewish traits such as a
beard and a skullcap
are patently lacking.
Stipple engraving,
contemporary, by
Wilhelm Arndt
(d. 1809).

performed in closed circles, at the home he shared with his wife Henriette Herz – a highly regarded woman of culture in her own right. The notoriety he gained through his popular presentations was enhanced by the books and essays he wrote on medicine and philosophy for a German public. In his *Versuch über den Geschmack und die Ursachen seiner Verschiedenheit* (Essay on taste and on the causes of its variety) he addressed an ongoing debate about aesthetics, directly engaging with the views that prominent figures such as Herder and Kant had recently expressed on these subjects. On another occasion he intervened in a medical and philosophical controversy that emerged after the discovery of vaccination in 1796. In *Über die Brutalimpfung und deren Vergleichung mit der humanen* (On the animal vaccine and its comparison to the human one), a text written in 1801 as an open letter to his German colleague Dohmeyer, the personal physician to an English prince, Herz condemned the newly introduced practice of compulsory vaccination, articulating a position that placed him in the minority camp and ended up harming his reputation.

Probably the most remarkable case of a Jewish intellectual participating in the German public sphere is that of Salomon Maimon (1753–1800), a talented Lithuanian scholar and Talmudist who underwent an astonishing transformation and became a recognized German philosopher of the Enlightenment. His case represents a rare instance in which the activity of a Jewish intellectual in the European public sphere arose largely as an alternative to his activity within the Jewish world, after failing to establish himself in the modern Jewish republic of letters. As Maimon described in his famous autobiography (*Lebensgeschichte*), published in two volumes in 1792–93, in his thirst for knowledge, and having developed a defiant anticlerical stance vis-à-vis the rabbinical elite to which he had aspired to belong in his youth, he left behind his wife and son and fled the life he abhorred in what he perceived as his dark homeland. Upon his arrival in Germany, he was able to overcome the difficult obstacles of penury, solitude and the lack

of formal education, and he acquired knowledge of German and European culture in a largely autodidactic manner.

Equipped with a vast knowledge of science and a sharp mind, he then tried to enter the ranks of the maskilim and join their efforts by engaging in literary activity intended for the Haskalah's target audience. With this purpose in mind he cooperated with the maskilim in Berlin, where he spent many years and prepared several books in Hebrew for publication. Some were published, but most were not, as was the case with *Ta'alumot hokhmah* (Mysteries of Science, 1787), a very up-to-date physics book in Hebrew which lucidly explained Newton's theory. This book was meant to contribute to the maskilic effort of disseminating knowledge and rationalizing Jewish culture, especially addressing the Jews of Poland, who were believed to be submerged in ignorance. But the fact that it remained

FIGURE 61A
As Salomon Maimon states at the end of the first volume of his *Lebensgeschichte*, his move from east to west was prescribed by the dictates of reason: confronted by fanaticism in his native land, he decided to go to Berlin and rid himself of any sign of superstition through the means of Enlightenment.

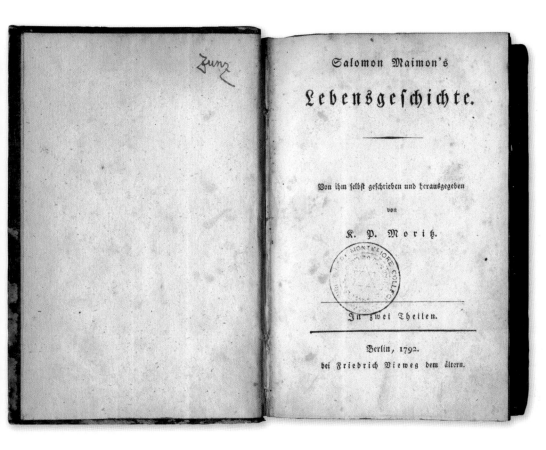

in manuscript makes evident Maimon's failure to participate actively in the Haskalah project and the failure of the maskilim to recognize Maimon's immense potential and employ his talents to advance their goals. Frustrated by this turn of events, Maimon sought intellectual satisfaction elsewhere. The impressive list of works he authored in the last decade of his life reflect an outpouring of philosophical creativity whose speculative topics showed no special interest in Jewish matters, but, rather, constitute a valuable contribution to the German republic of letters. It is significant that even his autobiography, which depicts his liberation as a Jew from dependence on rabbinical authority and his free use of reason, was written in German, edited by Karl Philipp Moritz, a Christian friend and colleague, and addresses mainly a non-Jewish audience.

FIGURE 61B
Ta'alumot hokhmah by Sh'lomo ben Rabbi Y'hudah of Lithuania (Salomon Maimon), composed at Breslau in the year 5547 (1787).

CHAPTER 8

Beyond Haskalah:
radicalization in Jewish intellectual circles

MAIMON'S ESTRANGEMENT from the Jewish public sphere was indicative of a process that had started earlier in the eighteenth century and was becoming more extreme in the 1790s, especially in Berlin. There now emerged a group of freethinkers in Jewish society who maintained an affinity for the values and concepts of the European Enlightenment but were only partially attached to the Haskalah. At the top of their agenda were issues such as the integration of Jews into German society and culture and their acceptance as citizens of the state – a theme that had re-emerged with greater impetus in public debate after the death of the Prussian King Frederick II in 1786 and in the wake of the French Revolution in 1789. Like the earlier maskilim, these radical maskilim also criticized aspects of Jewish life and Judaism; but there were important differences. Their criticism was now far more comprehensive than before, and it reflected more than hitherto the negative views of Judaism and the Jews held by Gentiles. Furthermore, the members of the new elite distanced themselves from the Jewish masses and established a clear distinction between the latter and themselves. They claimed that they represented a new type of reformed Jew that was emerging in German lands, and especially in the Prussian capital, a type which radically differed from the superstitious, backward masses, and which, unlike the latter, was capable of becoming a worthy citizen of the state.

A typical representative of the process of alienation from Jewish society and religion that was becoming more and more visible among Berlin Jewish intellectuals was Lazarus Ben-david. Like Marcus Herz and many other Jewish contemporar-ies, Bendavid was an adherent of Kantian philosophy, which

FIGURE 62 Portrait of Lazarus Bendavid.

he popularized through writings and lectures in his native Berlin and in Vienna, where he spent several years of his life. Bendavid was a prolific and extremely dynamic intellectual. He was active in numerous enlightened German societies and even presided over some of them. He printed articles in major journals in Prussia and the Habsburg Empire, and published a considerable number of books dealing with philosophy, mathematics – such as his *Versuch einer logischen Auseinandersetzung des Mathematischen Unendlichen* (Attempt at a logical analysis of mathematical infinity) of 1789 – and Jewish issues. Among the works devoted to Jewish matters was *Sammlung der Schriften an die Nationalversammlung* (Collection of texts submitted to the National Assembly), published in 1789 following the French Revolution, a German translation of texts presented to the National Assembly in Paris by French Jews concerning the amelioration of their civil status.

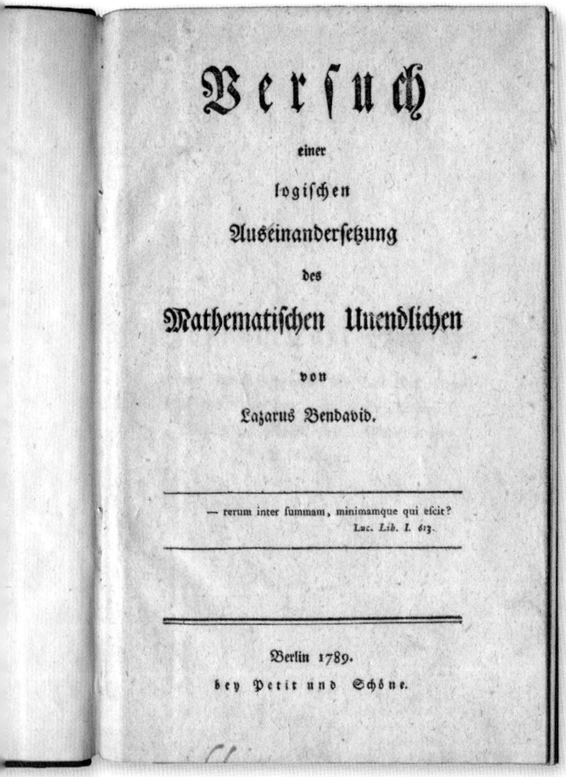

Versuch
einer
logischen
Auseinandersetzung
des
Mathematischen Unendlichen
von
Lazarus Bendavid.

— rerum inter ſummam, minimamque qui eſcit?
Luc. Lib. I. 613.

Berlin 1789.
bey Petit und Schöne.

FIGURE 63
Lazarus Bendavid's *Versuch einer logischen Auseinandersetzung des Mathematischen Unendlichen*.

In common with other members of the new Jewish intelligentsia, Bendavid voiced radical criticism of Judaism and the Jews to the point of blaming the latter for their insularity and their negative image, and holding Talmudic and rabbinical Judaism, along with the practical commandments, responsible for the purported social and cultural perversion of his co-religionists. In view of this harsh criticism, Bendavid tried to define his own place within Jewish society, drawing internal boundaries based on an ideological cross-section and the level of acculturation of different Jews. In his controversial treatise of 1793 *Etwas zur Charackteristick der Juden* (Notes regarding the characteristics of the Jews), he characterized four groups that, in his view, made up contemporary Jewish society as it faced the challenges of modernization: the majority group of

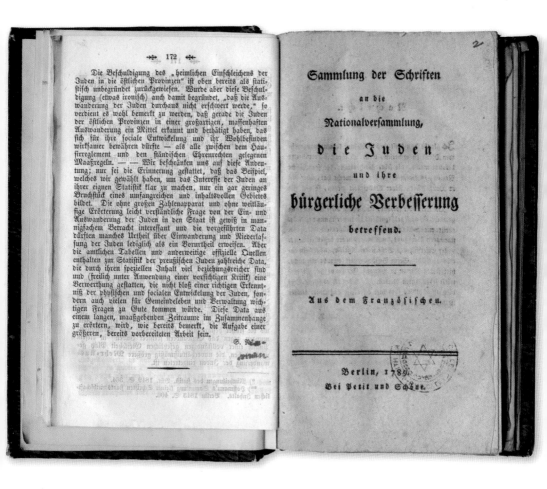

Die Beschuldigung des „heimlichen Einschleichens der
Juden in die östlichen Provinzen" ist oben bereits als stati-
stisch unbegründet zurückgewiesen. Wurde aber diese Beschuldigung (etwas ironisch) auch damit begründet, „daß die Auswanderung der Juden durchaus nicht erschwert werde," so
verdient es wohl bemerkt zu werden, daß gerade die Juden
der östlichen Provinzen in einer großartigen, massenhaften
Auswanderung ein Mittel erkannt und bethätigt haben, das
sich für ihre sociale Entwickelung als ein Wohlbefinden
wirksamer bewähren dürfte — als alle zwischen dem Hau-
sirreglement und den ständischen Ehrenrechten gelegenen
Maaßregeln. — — Wir beschränken uns auf diese Andeu-
tung; nur sei die Erinnerung gestattet, daß das Beispiel,
welches wir gewählt haben, um das Interesse der Juden an
ihrer eignen Statistik klar zu machen, nur ein gar geringes
Bruchstück eines umfangreichen und inhaltsvollen Gebietes
bildet. Die oben große Zahlenapparat und ohne weitläu-
fige Erörterung leicht verständliche Frage von der Ein- und
Auswanderung der Juden in den Staat ist gewiß in man-
nigfachem Betracht interessant und die vorgeführten Data
dürften manches Urtheil über Einwanderung und Niederlas-
sung der Juden lediglich als ein Vorurtheil erweisen. Aber
die amtlichen Tabellen und anderweitige officielle Quellen
enthalten zur Statistik der preußischen Juden zahlreiche Data,
die durch ihren speziellen Inhalt viel beziehungsreicher sind
und (freilich unter Anwendung einer vorsichtigen Kritik) eine
Verwerthung gestatten, die nicht bloß einer richtigen Erkennt-
niß der physischen und socialen Entwickelung der Juden, sondern auch vielen für Gemeindeleben und Verwaltung wich-
tigen Fragen zu Gute kommen würde. Diese Data aus
einem langen, maaßgebenden Zeitraume im Zusammenhange
zu erörtern, wird, wie bereits bemerkt, die Aufgabe einer
größeren, bereits vorbereiteten Arbeit sein.

S. R——

Sammlung der Schriften

an die

Nationalversammlung,

die Juden

und ihre

bürgerliche Verbesserung

betreffend.

Aus dem Französischen.

Berlin, 1789.
Bei Petit und Schöne.

'unreformable' Jews, consisting of those totally faithful to the
religious tradition; the libertines who represented a vulgar modernization that was indifferent to enlightenment and morality
and disgraced decent Jews; the group of decent moral Jews
who still clung to unreformed Judaism and, though not yet
enlightened, had the potential of becoming so; and the small
group of 'truly enlightened', who were willing to revolutionize
their religious concepts and to abrogate the obligation of observ-
ing the commandments, without however developing religious
apathy. It was this last group, of which he saw himself as a
representative, which could best contribute to the improvement
of the character of the Jews, thereby enabling them to become
respectable subjects of the modern state.

Bendavid was Mendelssohn's admirer, but in his *Etwas zur
Charackteristick der Juden* he expressed an approach that was

FIGURE 64
*Sammlung der
Schriften an die
Nationalversammlung.*

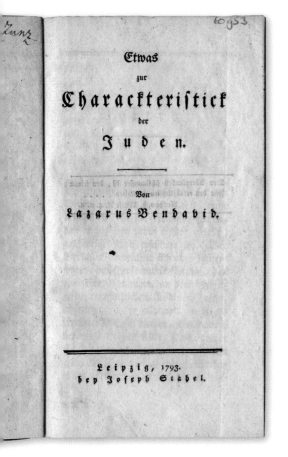

Etwas

zur

Charackteristick

der

Juden.

Von

Lazarus Bendavid.

Leipzig, 1793.
bey Joseph Stabel.

FIGURE 65
In *Etwas zur
Charackteristick der
Juden*, Bendavid
presented his radical
criticism of Jewish
society.

the exact opposite of Mendelssohn's and constituted a radicalization of earlier maskilic views. His was a Kantian approach – seeking in Jewish religion its inner moral essence and totally rejecting its rituals. Precisely ten years after Mendelssohn in *Jerusalem* had stated that the unique essence of Judaism lay in the obligation to observe the practical commandments, Bendavid put forth the radical idea of totally annulling the commandments as an essential step to ensure the existence of the Jews in the modern world.

Saul Ascher (1767–1822), another Berlin Jew, also took a step in contradiction to Mendelssohn's approach. In his *Leviathan oder Ueber Religion in Rücksicht des Judenthums* (Leviathan or On Religion in regard to Judaism) (1792), Ascher, a bookseller and publicist, proposed a religious reform as a prerequisite for acceptance of the Jews as full citizens of the state. Following Kant, he also stated that the law-based character of Judaism was opposed to the 'true autonomy of the will', and irrelevant to the new generation. In contrast to Mendelssohn, Ascher proposed a list of dogmas as an obligatory basis for the Jewish religion – a new set of laws that would preserve the essence of the religion and relinquish its traditional form.

Ascher, however, did more than call for the radical transformation of Judaism and the Jews. He was among the few Jewish-German intellectuals of his time who dared to engage in a direct confrontation with contemporary foes of the Jews. Since the 1790s and well into the nineteenth century, Ascher had courageously rejected anti-Jewish claims of a new, modern nature, based no longer on religious but on political arguments. In *Eisenmenger der Zweite* (The Second Eisenmenger), for instance, a pamphlet of 1794, Ascher refuted the denigration of

Judaism and the Jews as preached by Johann Gottlieb Fichte, the well-known German philosopher, and to some extent by Kant. In the previous year, Fichte had accused the Jews of being a state within a state, a misanthropic group, guilty of its own segregation within society, and had therefore denied them the entitlement to civil and political rights, claiming that granting citizenship to this depraved people would be disastrous to German society. In a famous passage Fichte affirmed that the perverted ideas of Judaism were so fixed in the Jews that they could only be eradicated if Jews were beheaded and granted a new head instead. In a harsh reply, Ascher rejected Fichte's claims against the Jews one by one, and accused the German thinker of promoting a new brand of Jew-hatred by reformulating old prejudices in a modern form, using secular arguments largely based on Kantian philosophy. As someone who fostered

FIGURE 66
Saul Ascher's
Leviathan, a proposal
for the religious
reform of Judaism.

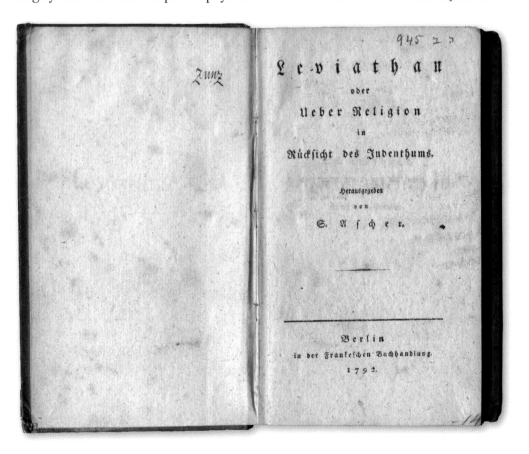

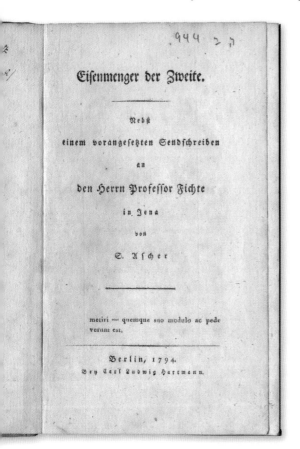

the ancient hostility towards the Jews, Fichte deserved to be called the Second Eisenmenger after the ill-famed author of *Entdecktes Judenthum* (Judaism Unmasked), a classic and very influential polemic against Judaism written in 1700.

Wolf Davidson (1772–1800) was another spokesperson for Jewry in the German public sphere. In 1798 this enlightened Jew from Berlin published his *Ueber die bürgerliche Verbesserung der Juden* (On the Civil Improvement of the Jews), a work bearing the same title as Dohm's book published seventeen years earlier and intended, like its predecessor, to foster the amelioration of the status of the Jews, although reaching different conclusions. As earlier maskilim, Davidson also bemoaned the escalating acculturation and the ostentatious behaviour of the Berlin Jewish bourgeoisie. However, he also saw grounds for celebration, writing with pride about the emergence of a diversified and impressive group of freethinking Jews, many of them artists or members of the free professions, dispersed in various Prussian cities but residing mainly in Berlin. He counted about forty men and women, some of them outstanding figures in their fields, who were socially and economically integrated into German society and, in Davidson's opinion, had made a significant contribution to Jewish prestige. In view of the success of the German-Jewish intelligentsia in the overall public sphere, Davidson expected to see the Jews fully accepted into Christian society, and he called on the state to permit intermarriage between Jews and Christians without requiring their conversion. Addressing the new Prussian king, Friedrich Wilhelm III, and the German audience in general, he concluded his book with a fervent call for

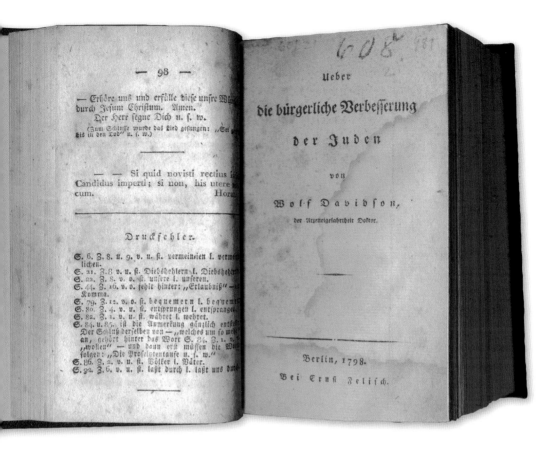

FIGURE 68
Ueber die bürgerliche Verbesserung der Juden, a defence of Jewish emancipation by Wolf Davidson, a physician from Berlin and an enlightened Jew.

maximum integration of the Jews as useful citizens of the state. He was expressing the wishes and aspirations of many radical members of the German-Jewish intelligentsia at the time, who had left aside former maskilic goals of internal change and were waging instead a political campaign in the general public arena to achieve civil rights.

Crisis and renewal at the turn of the nineteenth century

The last barrier that many members of the new Jewish intelligentsia declined to cross in their ambitious efforts to gain an entrance into German society was religious conversion to Christianity. Although the Haskalah's prominent spokesmen in the 1790s no longer hesitated to launch formidable anticlerical assaults on the rabbinical elite and even condemned the moderate

maskilim – who, unlike them, were unwilling to give up the commandments in exchange for legal emancipation – these deists still looked for a way to maintain a connection to the Jewish fold. However, this particular religious hurdle was also overcome at the very end of the century by none other than David Friedländer, a prominent maskil and one of the leading Jews in Prussia, in an act that reflects the profound crisis experienced by the Berlin Haskalah.

In 1799 this distinguished member of the Jewish community, who had played a major role in the Jewish Enlightenment and was then considered by many to be Mendelssohn's spiritual heir, anonymously sent a provocative letter to pastor Wilhelm Abraham Teller (1734–1804), a liberal proponent of rational religion and a leading member of the Protestant Church in Berlin, under the heading *Sendschreiben an Seine Hochwürden, Herrn Oberconsistorialrath und Probst Teller zu Berlin, von einigen Hausvätern jüdischer Religion* (Open Letter to His Most Worthy, Supreme Consistorial Counsellor and Provost Teller in Berlin, from some Householders of Jewish Religion). In the name of 'a number of heads of families of the Jewish religion', he made an extraordinary, unprecedented proposal: namely, that the Jewish elite be admitted to the Protestant Church, on the condition that they be allowed to do so simply by undergoing the ceremony of baptism only; that is, without accepting the Christian dogmas, which in Friedländer's opinion were hard to reconcile with reason and natural religion. In exchange, they would be granted civil and political rights.

Historians have argued over whether Friedländer's proposal reflects the alienation from Judaism of an opportunistic assimilationist who, speaking for a small group of wealthy Jews, envisioned the act of nominal conversion to Christianity as the entrance ticket to German society; or whether his proposal reflects the divided soul of an enlightened Jew who was torn between his emotive allegiance to the religion of his forefathers,

on the one hand, and his rational beliefs, on the other. Those who support the latter claim note that in his epistle Friedländer, rather than repudiating Judaism, was in fact defending its basic principles and the moral character of the Jews in front of his German audience. Whichever the case may be, it is easy to understand why Friedländer's letter to Teller provoked an immediate debate, involving Jews and Christians.

One of the most influential Christian replies came from Friedrich Schleiermacher (1768–1834), then a young theologian living in Berlin, who published anonymously his *Briefe bei Gelegenheit der politisch theologischen Aufgabe und des Sendschreibens jüdischer Hausväter* (Letters on the occasion of the political-theological task and the Open Letter of Jewish Householders) shortly after reading Friedländer's epistle. Another notable response was published by Teller himself as *Beantwortung des Sendschreibens einiger Hausväter jüdischer Religion an mich den Probst Teller* (Response to the Open Letter from some Householders of Jewish

FIGURE 70
Friendländer's controversial letter to Provost Teller, sent anonymously in 1799 in the name of a group of Jewish wealthy families.

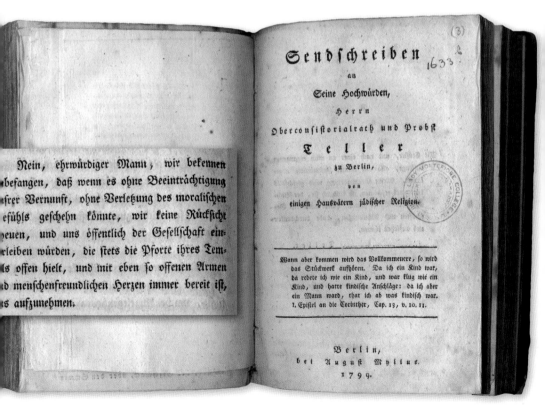

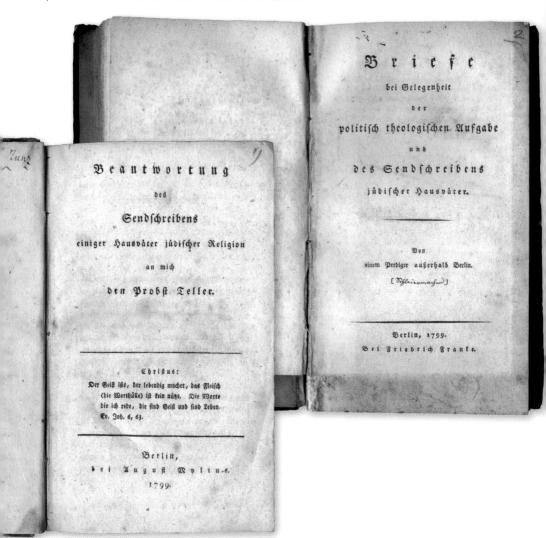

Briefe

bei Gelegenheit

der

politisch theologischen Aufgabe

und

des Sendschreibens

jüdischer Hausväter.

Von

einem Prediger außerhalb Berlin.

[*Schleiermacher*]

Berlin, 1799.
Bei Friedrich Frank.

Beantwortung

des

Sendschreibens

einiger Hausväter jüdischer Religion

an mich

den Probst Teller.

Christus:
Der Geist ist's, der lebendig machet, das Fleisch
(die Worthülle) ist kein nütze. Die Worte
die ich rede, die sind Geist und sind Leben.
Ev. Joh. 6, 63.

Berlin,
bei August Mylius.
1799.

FIGURES 71 & 72
Replies to
Friedländer's letter
by two Protestant
preachers,
Schleiermacher (*right*)
and Teller (*left*).

Religion to me, Provost Teller, Berlin 1799). Both Protestant preachers endorsed Friedländer's aspirations to ameliorate the civil and political status of the Jews and discussed his letter with all seriousness, but they turned down his proposal to undergo a merely nominal conversion to Christianity as an insincere act that would bring no benefit to the Christian Church.

Numerous texts surrounding Friedländer's anonymous proposal (which prompted a heated debate) were published in 1799–1800.

de es von mir anmaßend seyn, wenn ich ihr freies Urtheil ihnen streitig machen wollte. Nur ich hielt dafür, irgend eine Antwort der Humanität, dem in mich gesetzten Zutrauen, und der Sache selbst schuldig zu seyn, daß ich daher auch öffentlich sie versprach, um keiner Nachreue Raum zu geben. Sie selbst aber sei nun ausgefallen wie sie wolle, ihr Erfolg möge seyn der oder jener, so wird es mir so gar lieb seyn, recht viele noch so weit von dem meinigen abstimmende Urtheile darüber zu lesen und für mich in aller Stille den möglichsten guten Gebrauch davon zu machen. Lasset nur uns Alle, auch bei dieser Gelegenheit, dem nachstreben, was zum Frieden und zur Besserung untereinander dienet! Röm. 14, 9.

Beantwortung

des

an Herrn Probst Teller

erlassenen

Sendschreibens

einiger

Hausväter jüdischer Nation.

Nicht von

Teller.

Non quis, sed quid.

Berlin,
bei Friedrich Maurer, 1799.

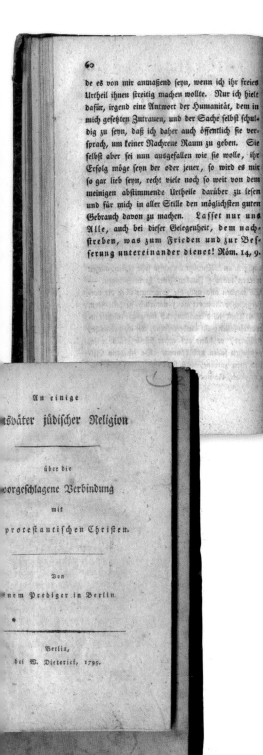

An einige
Hausväter jüdischer Religion

über die

vorgeschlagene Verbindung

mit

protestantischen Christen.

Von
einem Prediger in Berlin.

Berlin,
bei W. Dieterici, 1799.

FIGURE 73 (*above*)
Beantwortung des an Herrn Probst Teller erlassenen Sendschreibens einiger Hausväter jüdischer Nation / nicht von Teller (Response to the Open Letter sent to Provost Teller by some Householders of the Jewish Nation / not by Teller).

FIGURE 74 (*left*) *An einige Hausväter jüdischer Religion: über die vorgeschlagene Verbindung mit den protestantischen Christen / von einem Prediger in Berlin* (To some Householders of Jewish Religion: concerning the proposed connection with the Protestant Christians / by a Preacher in Berlin).

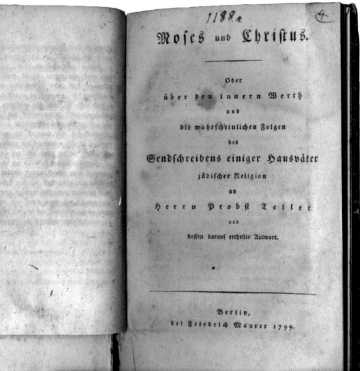

FIGURE 75 *Moses und Christus. Oder über den innern Werth und die wahrscheinlichen Folgen des Sendschreibens einiger Hausväter jüdischer Religion an Herrn Probst Teller und dessen darauf ertheilte Antwort* (Moses and Christ. Or on the intrinsic value and the likely consequences of the Open Letter of some Householders of Jewish Religion to Provost Teller and his answer), by Benjamin Gottlob Gerlach.

FIGURE 76 *Sollen sich die Christen beschneiden oder die Juden taufen lassen?* (Should Christians allow themselves to be circumcised or Jews to be baptized?), by Johann Christoph Vollbeding (b. 1757).

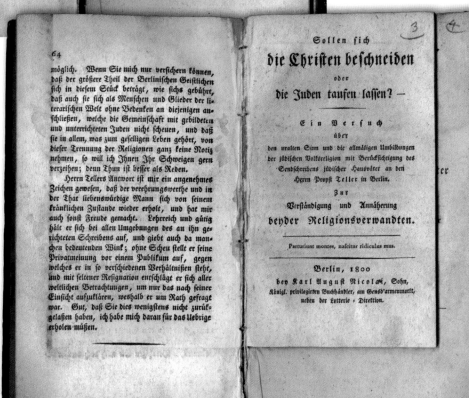

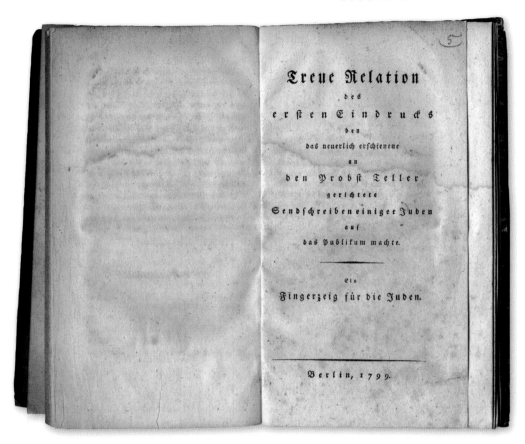

Treue Relation
des
ersten Eindrucks
den
das neuerlich erschienene
an
den Probst Teller
gerichtete
Sendschreiben einiger Juden
auf
das Publikum machte.

Ein
Fingerzeig für die Juden.

Berlin, 1799.

More telling was the reaction of moderate maskilim. They were astounded to find Friedländer committing an act that in their view amounted to a betrayal of the nation and an irresponsible derailment of the Haskalah revolution. Not without reason, Friedländer's letter to Teller has been taken as the symbolic end of the Berlin Haskalah. By the time it was written, the organized movement had largely collapsed. For the young Haskalah movement, the century came to a close in a series of strident, worrisome chords, attended by a profound sense of crisis. The struggle to change the legal status of Prussian Jewry had been disappointing and futile, and it was accompanied by voices expressing deep alienation from tradition and the Jewish community. Internal quarrels among the modern intelligentsia between moderates and radicals and between reformists and assimilationists impeded the momentum of the

FIGURE 77 *Treue Relation des ersten Eindrucks den das neuerlich erschienene an den Probst Teller gerichtete Sendschreiben einiger Juden auf das Publikum machte: ein Fingerzeig für die Juden* (Reliable account of the first impression which the recently published Open Letter by some Jews to Provost Teller made on the public: a hint to the Jews).

Erneuerte Gesetze für die Lehrlinge
der jüdischen Freyschule zu Berlin.

1, Die Lehrstunden werden Nachmittags von 2 bis 7 gehalten, in welchen im Schreiben, Rechnen, Buchhalten, Zeichnen, Lesen, deutscher und französischer Sprache, auch Geographie Unterricht gegeben wird.

2, Die Lehrlinge müssen die Lehrstunden fleißig und unausgesetzt besuchen, und geschiehet es, daß jemand 3 mal hintereinander, oder auch nur in derselben Woche ohne hinlängliche Ursache ausbleibt: so wird dieses den Eltern oder Vorgesetzten angezeigt, und der Lehrling verliert bei Wiederholung dieser Nachläßigkeit den Unterricht, dessen er sich unwürdig gemacht.

3, Jeder Lehrling, der an dieser oder jener Stunde Theil nimmt, muß sich gleich im Anfange derselben einfinden; bleibt er eine viertel Stunde aus, so wird er für dieses mal gar nicht zugelassen, läßt er sich dieses Versehen noch einmal zu Schulden kommen, so gilt die Strafe des 2ten.

4, Ein jeder Lehrling muß sich der Reinlichkeit, so wohl in seinen Kleidern, sie mögen übrigens neu oder alt seyn, als in Ansehung seines Körpers, des Kopfes, der Hände und dergleichen befleißigen, welches er so wohl den Lehrern, als den Mitschülern schuldig ist, und übrigens still bescheiden auf und ab gehen, Lehrern und Vorgesetzten in allen folgsam und gehorsam seyn.

5, Aus eben diesem Grunde darf niemand während des Unterrichts weder mit seinem Nachbarn plaudern, noch essen, noch überhaupt etwas von dem thun, was ihn oder die andern Schüler in der Aufmerksamkeit stört, welche sie dem Unterricht widmen müssen. In jedem Uebertretungs=Fall wird so gleich eine verhältnißmäßige Strafe, und bei fortdauerndem Ungehorsam die gänzliche Verweisung aus der Schule erfolgen.

6, Jedem jüdischen Feyer und Fasttage, worunter auch Renmonde begriffen sind, bleibt die Schule geschlossen, und dieses sind alsdenn die Ferien, so wie diese in allen übrigen Schulen üblich sind.

ערנייערטע געזעצע פֿיר דיא לעהרלינע דער יודישן פֿרײשולע אין בערלין ׃

1. דיא לעהרשטונדן ווערדן נאבֿמיטטאגס פֿאן ‎2 ביז ‎7. געהאלטן ׀ אין וועלֿן אים שרײבן ׀ רעֿנן ׀ בוֿהאלט ׀ צײֿנען ׀ לעזן ׀ דײטשער אונד פֿראנצעזישער שפראֿע ׀ אויֿ יעאגראפֿיא אונטעריֿט געגעבן ווירד ׃

2. דיא לעהרלינע מיסן דיא לעהרשטונדן פֿלײסיג אונאויסגעזעצט בעזוֿן ׀ אונד געשיהט עס ׀ דאס יעמאר דרײא מאהל ֿינטעראײנאנדר ׀ אדר אויֿ נור אן דערזעלבן וואֿע אהנע הינלענגליֿע אורזאֿע אויס בלײבט ׃ זא ווירד דיזעם דען עלטערן ארר פֿארגעזעצט אנגעצײגט ׀ אונד דער לעהרלינג פֿערליהרט בײא ווידרהאלונג דיזר נאֿלעסיגקייט דען אונטעריֿט דעסן ער זיֿ אונגעווירדיג געמאֿט ׃

3. יעדר לעהרלינג ׀ דער אן דיזער אדר יענר שטונדֿ טהייל נימט ׀ מוס זיֿ גלײֿ אים אנבֿאנגע דערזעלֿב אײנפֿינדֿן ׀ בלײבט ער אײנע פֿירטעלשטונדע אויס זא ווירד ער פֿיר דיזעם מאהל גאר ניֿט צולאסן לעסט ער זיֿ דיזעם פֿערזעהן נאֿאײנמאהל צו שולֿד קאמן ׀ זא גילט דיא שטראֿפֿע דעם ‎2.

4. אײן יעדר לעהרלינג מוס זיֿ דער רײנליֿקייט ׀ זא וואהל אין זײן קלײדרן ׀ זיא מעגן איבריגענס נײא אדר אלֿט זײן ׀ אלס אין אנזעהונג זײנעס קערפֿערס ארם דעם קאפֿֿפֿ ׀ דער הענדע אונד דער גלײֿן בֿלײסיגן ׀ וועלֿֿעס ער זא וואהל דען לעהרן ׀ אלס דען מיטשולערן ׀ שולדיג איזט ׀ אונר איבריגענס שטיל בעשיירן אויֿ אונד אבגעהן ׀ לעהרן אונד פֿארגעזעצט אין אלן פֿאלגזאם אונר געהאראם זײן ׃

5. אויס עבן דיזעם גרונדע דארֿף נימאנד וועהרענדר דעם אונטעריֿטס וועדר מיט זײנעם נאבֿבאר פֿליודרן ׀ נאֿ עסן ׀ נאֿ איבערהויפֿט עטוואס פֿאן דעם טהון ׀ וואס איהן אדר דיא אנדרן שילר אין דער אויֿמערקזאמקייט שטערהרט ׀ וועלֿֿע זיא דעם אונטעריֿֿט ווידמן מיסן ׃ אין יעדם איבֿערטרעטונגספֿאל ווירד זאגלײֿ אײנע פֿערהעלטניס מעסיגע שטראֿפֿע ׀ אונר בײא פֿארטדֿורנדם אונ געהאראם דיא גענצליֿע פֿערווײזונג אויס דער שולֿ ערפֿאלגן ׃

6. יעדעם יודישן פֿײער אונד פֿאסטטאגע ׀ וואראונטר אויֿ נײמאנעד בגריֿפֿן זינד ׀ בלײבט דיא שולע געשלאסן ׀ אונד דיזעם זינד אלם דען פֿעריען ׀ זא וויא דיזע אין אלן איבריגן שולן איבליֿ זינד ׃

7, Damit die Lehrlinge Gelegenheit erhalten, die Fortschritte, welche sie in den Wissenschaften gemacht haben, zu zeigen, und durch die Ehre, welche ihnen dafür zu Theil wird, eine Aufmunterung für die Zukunft zu haben, so sollen jährlich zwey Privat, und Eine öffentliche Prüfung gehalten werden. Das Privat-Examen geschiehet in Gegenwart der Direction und der Lehrer, und zwar

Ende des Monaths Adars
und Ende „ „ Elluls

Das öffentliche aber wird einige Tage nach dem Privatexamen zu Ende Adars vorgenommen. Außer der Ehre, welche die fleißigen unter den Lehrlingen erwartet, sollen sie auch noch anderweitig belohnet werden; besonders durch die besten Zeugnisse, durch Empfehlungen, welche zu ihrem Fortkommen in der Welt beitragen, u. s. w. Jedoch wird hiebey nicht auf die erworbenen Kenntnisse allein, sondern auch sehr auf das sittliche Betragen in der Schule Rücksicht genommen, und soll das zuertheilende Lob darnach eingerichtet werden.

8, Bey dem geringen Beytrag, welchen die vermögendere Zöglinge zur Unterhaltung der Schule zu leisten haben, darf man wohl verlangen, daß er gehörig und zur rechten Zeit abgeliefert werde. Wenn daher die Quitung darüber dem Lehrer nicht am Tage nach Verlauf eines Monaths vorgezeiget werden kann, so muß der Schüler bis zur Beybringung derselben wegbleiben, und wenn diese sich bis zum 14ten verzögert, so ist er aus dem Register der Lehrlinge ausgestrichen. Die monathlichen Beyträge erstrecken sich auf jeden Monath im Jahre, es mögen in denselben Feyer oder Fasttage gewesen seyn, und die Strafe im ausbleibenden Falle, bleibt immer dieselbe.

Berlin den 1sten December 1796.

Direction der jüdischen Freyschule.

I. D. Itzig.

7. דאמיט דיא לעהרלינגע גלעגענהייט ערהאלטן, דיא
פארטשריטטע, וועלכע זיא אין דען וויסענשאפטן
געמאכט האבן, צו צייגן, אונד דורך דיא עהרע,
וועלכע איהנן דאפיר צו טהייל ווירד, איינע אויפ=
מונטרונג פיר דיא צוקונפט צו האבן, זא זאללן יעהר=
ליך צוויא פריפאט, אונד איינע עפפענטליכע פריפונג
געהאלטן ווערדן. דאס פריפאט עקסאמן געשיהט אין
געגענווארט דער דירעקציאהן אונד דער לעהרר, אונד
צוואר ענדע דעם מאנאטס אדר אונד אלול.
דאס עפפענטליכע אבר ווירד איינגע טאגע נאך דעם
פריפאט עקסאמן צו ענדע אדר פארגנאמן. אויסר
דער עהרע וועלכער דיא פלייסיגן אונטר דען לעהר=
לינגן ערווארטט, זאלן זיא אויך נאך אנדערווייטיג
בלאהנט ווערדן; בזאנדרס דורך דיא בעסטן צייג=
ניסע, דורך עמפפעהלונגן, וועלכע צו איהרם פארט=
קאממן אין דער וועלט בייטראגן א. ז. וו. יעדאך
ווירד היאבייא ניכט אויף דיא ערווארבנן קענטניססע
אלליין, זאנדרן אויך זעהר אויף דאס זיטליכע
בטראגן אין דער שולע ריקזיכט גנאמן, אונד זאלל דאס
צו ערטהיילענדע לאב דארנאך איינגריכטט ווערדן.

8. בייא דעם גרינגן בייטראג, וועלכן דיא פרמעגנרע
צעגלינגע צור אונטרהאלטונג דער שולע צו לייסטן
האבן, דארף מאן וואהל פרלאנגן, דאס ער געהעריג
אונד צור רעכטן צייט אבגליפרט ווערדע. ווען דא=
הער דיא קוויטטונג דאריבר דעם לעהרר ניכט אם
טאגע נאך פרלויף איינס מאנאטס פארגעצייגט ווערדן
קאן; זא מוס דער שילר ביס צור בייברינגונג דער=
זעלבן וועגבלייבן, אונד ווען דיזע זיך ביס צום 14 טען
פרצעגרט, זא איזט ער אויס דעם רעגיסטר
דער לעהרלינגע אויסגשטריכן. דיא מאנאטליכן
בייטרעגע ערשטרעקן זיך אויף יעדן מאנאט אים
יאהרע, עס מעגן אין דעמזעלבן פייער אדר פאסט=
טאגע גוועזן זיין, אונד דיא שטראפע אים אויסבלייבנדן
פאללע בלייבט אימער דיזעלבע.

ברלין ר״ח כסליו תקנ״ז לפ״ק.

דירעקציאהן דער יודישן
פריישולע.

איצק בר״ד.

maskilic republic at the very time when the orthodox protest was
growing stronger. The optimistic belief of the maskilim that the
Jewish public sphere could be reshaped by modern intellectuals
was replaced by their anxiety in the face of the secularization
gaining in momentum among the Jewish bourgeoisie in urban
communities – a process neither intended by the maskilim nor
controlled by them. Frustrated maskilim left the movement. The
closure of *ha-Me'asef* and the disbanding of the largest maskilic
society in 1797 marked, more than anything, the collapse of the
movement. It would be true to say that the end of the eighteenth
century brought with it the end of the first chapter in the history
of the Jewish Enlightenment movement.

But this was a promising end. Although the sweeping processes of modernization hardly left room for the trends of the
cultural renaissance of Hebrew literature led by the maskilim,
parallel to the descent of the Haskalah, steps were being taken in
Berlin itself to revive Jewish life and even to foster some of the
maskilic ideals in a new era. In the waning years of the eighteenth century and at the beginning of the nineteenth century,
attempts were made in the field of education to shape a new
generation of young Jews according to modern ideals. After a
period of troubled times, efforts were soon under way to instil
new life into the Jewish Free School in Berlin, as reflected in
numerous school reports – *Zweite Nachricht von dem Zustande
der jüdischen Freischule in Berlin* (Second Report of the Board of
the Jewish Free School in Berlin), Berlin 1804; *Dritte Nachricht
von dem Zustande der jüdischen Freischule in Berlin* (Third Report
of the Board of the Jewish Free School in Berlin), Berlin 1809
– and in the new statutes for the pupils, *Erneuerte Gesetze für die
Lehrlinge der jüdischen Freyschule zu Berlin* (Renewed regulations
for the pupils of the Jewish Free School in Berlin), signed by
Isaac Daniel Itzig in 1796. Initiatives were launched to establish
new schools in Berlin, now also catering for the modern education of Jewish girls. Evidence of this may be seen, for example,
in the programme for a new institution published by Moses Bock

in 1808, *Ankündigung einer Lehr- und Bildungsanstalt für Töchter
jüdischer Familien* (Announcement of a school for girls from
Jewish families). Also *ha-Me'asef,* which had previously suffered

7.
8.

Zweite Nachricht
von dem Zustande
der
jüdischen Freischule
in Berlin.

Womit
zu der öffentlichen Prüfung,
welche
in der Schulwohnung, Klosterstraße No. 35,
Dienstag den 8ten und Mittwoch den 9ten
Mai 1804 Vormittags von 9 und Nachmittags von halb drei Uhr an
veranstaltet werden soll,
die wohlthätigen Theilnehmer an
dieser Stiftung,
die resp. Eltern und Vorgesetzte unsrer Lehrlinge,
wie auch
alle Beschützer, Freunde und Gönner des Schulwesens ehrerbietigst einladen
der Direktor, die Inspektoren und die
Lehrer der jüdischen Freischule.

Berlin,
gedruckt bei Gottfried Hayn.
1804.

---

27) Ein Lehrling der 3. französischen Klasse, Joseph Gerson Jakob aus Meserig in Südpreußen,
rezitirt französisch das Lob der französischen
Sprache von la Touche.
28) Die zweite Rechenklasse. Lehrer Hr. Beschütz.
29) Die zweite geogr. Klasse. Lehrer Hr. Garlipp.
30) Ein Lehrling der 2. deutschen Klasse, Moses
Isaak aus Frankfurt a. d. O., rezitirt eine Fabel.

Nachmittags.

31) Ein Lehrling der 2. naturhistorischen Klasse,
Salomon Ephraim aus Berlin, rezitirt die Idylle
von Kleist: Iris.
32) Die mathem. Klasse. Lehrer Hr. Müller.
33) Ein Lehrling der 3. franz. Klasse, Abraham
Baba aus Berlin, rezitirt ein Fragment über
Voltaire als dramatischen Schriftsteller.
34) Ein Lehrling der 2. naturhistorischen Klasse,
Abraham Michel aus Neustadt-Eberswalde, rezitirt eine Stelle aus Kleists Frühling.
35) Zwei Lehrlinge der 1. deutschen Klasse, die sich
beide während ihres Aufenthalts auf unsrer Schule die
Achtung und die Liebe aller ihrer Lehrer und Mitschüler
erworben haben, nämlich Israel Jakob und Wilhelm Wegener, beide aus Berlin, nehmen in selbst
verfertigten Reden Abschied.
36) Censur aller Lehrlinge nach ihrer Folge in den
vier deutschen Klassen, und Vertheilung der Prämien
an die fleißigsten und gesittetsten Lehrlinge.
  Die jüdischen, deutschen und lateinischen Probe-
schriften und die Probezeichnungen der Lehrlinge werden an beiden Tagen vorgelegt werden.

  Zu dieser Schulfeierlichkeit laden der Direktor,
die Inspektores und die Lehrer der Schule die wohlthätigen Beförderer und Theilnehmer an unsrer Stiftung, die resp. Eltern und Vorgesetzten unsrer Lehrlinge und alle Kenner, Freunde und Gönner des
Schulwesens hierdurch ehrerbietigst ein.

Dritte Nachricht

von dem

Zustande der jüdischen Freischule
in Berlin.

Womit

zur öffentlichen Prüfung,
welche
in dem Fließchen Hause, Spandauer
Straße No. 21, Mittwoch den 3ten May, Vormittags
von 9 bis 12 und Nachmittags von 2 bis 5 Uhr gehalten
werden soll,

ehrerbietigst einladet

L. Bendavid,
zeitiger Direktor der Schule.

Berlin, 1809.

a decline in the number of subscriptions, leading first to irregular publication and then to complete closure, was revived.

Furthermore, the ideas, programmes and literary works of the Haskalah resonated in communities in which the processes of modernization were relatively slow or had not yet begun. Throughout the nineteenth century, centres of the Haskalah movement were established in the Austrian Empire (Vienna, Prague) and with special intensity in European communities, first in Galicia and then in the Russian Empire. There, the obstacles encountered along the way to Enlightenment were different from those prevalent in Germany. Galician maskilim regarded the pietistic movement of Hasidism as the major impediment to the modernization of the Jews, describing it as a troubling deviation in Jewish history, one that perpetuated the ignorance of the masses, fostered superstition and blocked progress.

From a historical perspective, it seems as if the whole public culture of the Jews in the modern age – the book culture, the

FIGURE 82
Announcement of the establishment of a new institution for the education of Jewish girls from 1808.

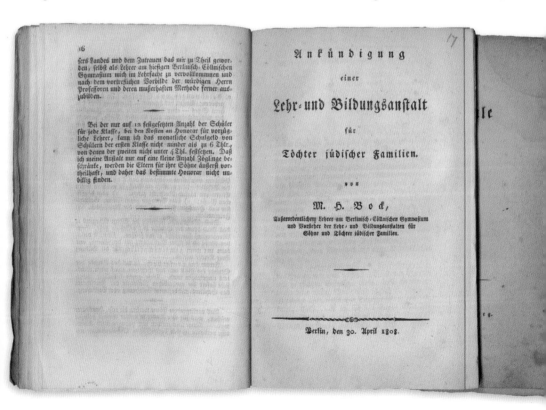

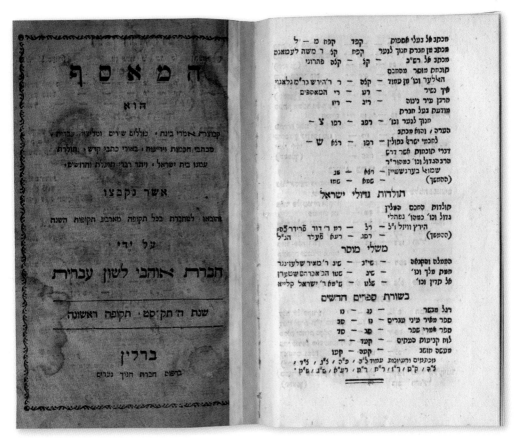

ideological debates, the new religious movements, modern
politics, the press as a forum of cultural and political discourse
– would not have been possible had it not been for that revolutionary breakthrough of a new Jewish intelligentsia. These
intellectuals expanded cultural boundaries, raised acute questions about the place of Jews in modern Europe and entered
into a cultural conflict with an emerging orthodox elite. This
revolution had many remarkable implications. New publications were added to the traditional Jewish library – books of
science, history, geography, language and philosophy. The
religious control over knowledge was weakened and in many
places changed hands. It was in this way that the Haskalah
played a key role in the transition of European Jewry from its
pre-modern, traditional stage to modernity, leaving a deep and
long-lasting imprint on Jewish life.

FIGURE 83
The 1808 edition
of the revived
ha-Me'asef.

Books and pamphlets from the Leopold Müller Memorial Library and the Bodleian Library

Ascher, Saul, *Eisenmenger der Zweite: nebst einem vorangesetzen Sendschreiben an den Herrn Professor Fichte in Jena*, Berlin: Hartmann, 1794. (Foyle–Montefiore Collection/Müller Library: Mont 60g28) FIGURE 67
——*Leviathan oder Ueber Religion in Rücksicht des Judenthums*, Berlin: Frankesche Buchhandlung, 1792. (Foyle–Montefiore Collection/Müller Library: Mont 60g29) FIGURE 66
Beantwortung des an Herrn Probst Teller erlassenen Sendschreibens einiger Hausväter jüdischer Nation/nicht von Teller, Berlin: Maurer, 1799. (Foyle–Montefiore Collection/Müller Library: Mont 60h1(2)) FIGURE 73
Behr, Isaschar (Isachar) Falkensohn, *Gedichte von einem pohlnischen Juden*, Mietau, Leipzig: Hinz, 1772. (Foyle–Montefiore Collection/Müller Library: Mont 58b45) FIGURE 53
Bendavid, Lazarus, *Dritte Nachricht von dem Zustande der jüdischen Freischule in Berlin*, Berlin: 1809. (Foyle–Montefiore Collection/Müller Library: Mont Misc. X-3) FIGURE 81
——*Etwas zur Charackteristick der Juden*, Leipzig: Stahel, 1793. (Foyle–Montefiore Collection/Müller Library: Mont 60g53) FIGURE 65
——*Sammlung der Schriften an die Nationalversammlung, die Juden und ihre bürgerliche Verbesserung betreffend*, Berlin: Petit und Schöne, 1789. (Foyle–Montefiore Collection/Müller Library: Mont Misc. XXVIII-2) FIGURE 64
——*Versuch einer logischen Auseinandersetzung des mathematischen Unendlichen*, Berlin: Petit und Schöne, 1789. (Foyle–Montefiore Collection/Müller Library: Mont 61b22) FIGURE 63
Ben Israel, Manasseh, *Rettung der Juden: aus dem Englischen übersetzt. Nebst einer Vorrede von Moses Mendelssohn*, Berlin, Stettin: Nicolai, 1782. (Foyle–Montefiore Collection/Müller Library: Mont 61b36) FIGURE 35
Bloch, Marcus Elieser, *Traité de la génération des vers des intestins et des vermifuges*, Strasbourg: Treuttel, 1788. (Bodleian–Oxford: Douce B 731; Radcliffe Science Library–Oxford: 1574 e.38)
Bock, Moses Hirsch, *Ankündigung einer Lehr- und Bildungsanstalt für Töchter jüdischer Familien*, Berlin: 1808. (Foyle–Montefiore Collection/Müller Library: Mont Misc. X-17) FIGURE 82
Cohen, Tobias, *Ma'aseh Tuviyah*, Venice: 1707–08. FIGURE 5
[Cranz, August], *Das Forschen nach Licht und Recht: in einem Schreiben an Herrn Moses Mendelssohn auf Veranlassung seiner merkwürdigen Vorrede zu Manasseh ben Israel*, Berlin: Maurer, 1782. (Foyle–Montefiore Collection/Müller Library: Mont 60h19) FIGURE 36
Davidson, Wolf, *Ueber die bürgerliche Verbesserung der Juden*, Berlin: Felisch, 1798. (Foyle–Montefiore Collection/Müller Library: Mont 60f21) FIGURE 68
Dohm, Christian Wilhelm, *Ueber die bürgerliche Verbesserung der Juden*, Berlin,

Stettin: Nicolai, 1783. (Foyle–Montefiore Collection/Müller Library: Mont 60g21) FIGURE 34

Euchel, Isaac, *Gebete der Juden*, Berlin: Vossische Buchhandlung, 1799. (Foyle–Montefiore Collection/Müller Library: Mont 63i23) FIGURE 45

Fichte, Johann Gottlieb, *Versuch einer Critik aller Offenbarung*, Königsberg: Hartung, 1792. (Foyle–Montefiore Collection/Müller Library: Mont 61b16) FIGURE 1

Friedländer, David, *Gebete der Juden*, Berlin: 546 (1785–86). (Foyle–Montefiore Collection/Müller Library: Mont 63j41) FIGURE 44

[Friedländer, David], *Sendschreiben an Seine Hochwürden, Herrn Oberconsistorialrath und Probst Teller zu Berlin*, Berlin: Mylius, 1799. (Foyle–Montefiore Collection/Müller Library: Mont 58Bh14(3)) FIGURE 70

Gans, David ben Solomon, *Sefer Nehmad ve-na'im: [...] 'al kelalot hokhmot ha-tevunah ve-kidush ha-hodesh u-medidot ha-kokhavim*, Y'esnits: (503) (1742–43). (Foyle–Montefiore Collection/Müller Library: Mont 61b12) FIGURE 9

Gedanken über Mosis Mendelssohns Jerusalem, in so fern diese Schrift dem Christenthum entgegen gesetzet ist, Bremen: Förster, 1786. (Foyle–Montefiore Collection/Müller Library: Mont 61b8 & 60f43) FIGURE 3

[Gerlach, Benjamin Gottlob], *Moses und Christus. Oder, über den innern Werth und die wahrscheinlichen Folgen des Sendschreibens einiger Hausväter jüdischer Religion an Herrn Probst Teller und dessen darauf ertheilte Antwort*, Berlin: Maurer, 1799. (Foyle–Montefiore/Müller Library: Mont 60f59) FIGURE 75

Hanau, Solomon Zalman ben Judah Loeb, ha-Kohen, *Sefer binyan Shelomoh: sheneim 'asar batim [...] meyusadim 'al adne yesod ha-dikduk*, Frankfurt am Main: 484 (1723–24). (Foyle–Montefiore Collection/Müller Library: Mont 63b11) FIGURE 13

—— *Sefer Tsohar ha-tevah: 'im mikhseh ha-tevah: kolel kol hokhmat ha-dikduk*, Dihrenfort: 547 (1786 or 1787). (Foyle–Montefiore Collection/Müller Library: Mont 63b14) FIGURE 14

Hannover, Raphael Levi, *Luhot ha-'ibur*, Leyden: Lissak, 516 (1755–56). (Foyle–Montefiore Collection/Müller Library: Mont 62e24))

Herz, Marcus, *D. Marcus Herz an den D. Dohmeyer über die Brutalimpfung und deren Vergleichung mit der humanen*, Berlin: Braun, 1801. (Foyle–Montefiore Collection/Müller Library: Mont 58Dg6) FIGURE 59

—— *Über die frühe Beerdigung der Juden*, Berlin: Orientalische Buchdruckerei, 1787. (Gedalyah Elkoshi Collection/Müller Library) FIGURE 57

—— *Versuch über den Geschmack und die Ursachen seiner Verschiedenheit*, Berlin: Voss, 1790. (Foyle–Montefiore Collection/Müller Library: Mont 62h12) FIGURE 58

Hurwitz, Judah ben Mordecai, ha-Levi, *Sefer 'Amude bet Yehudah: ha-'omdim le-Torah*, Amsterdam: 525 (1764 or 1765). (Foyle–Montefiore Collection/Müller Library: Mont 59b77) FIGURE 15

Immanuel, Ben Solomon, *Mahberot 'Imanu'el*, Berlin: Orientalische Buchdruckerei, 1796. (Foyle–Montefiore Collection/Müller Library: Mont 59b84) FIGURE 52

Israeli, Isaac ben Joseph, *Sefer yesod 'olam*, Berlin: 537 (1776–77). (Foyle–Montefiore Collection/Müller Library: Mont 62h6) FIGURE 12

Itzig, Isaac Daniel, *Erneuerte Gesetze für die Lehrlinge der jüdischen Freyschule zu Berlin*, Berlin: December 1796. (Foyle–Montefiore Collection/Müller Library: Mont Misc. X-1) FIGURES 78 & 79

Kant, Immanuel, 'Beantwortung der Frage: was ist Aufklärung?', in *Berlinische Monatsschrift*, Berlin: Haude und Spener, December 1784, pp. 481–94. (Foyle–Montefiore Collection/Müller Library: Mont 70e10) FIGURE 20

Lavater, Johann Caspar, *Antwort an den Herrn Moses Mendelssohn zu Berlin*, Berlin: Nicolai, 1770. (Foyle–Montefiore Collection/Müller Library: Mont 60h17) FIGURE 33

Lessing, Gotthold Ephraim, *Nathan der Weise: Ein dramatisches Gedicht in fünf Aufzügen*, Vienna: Kaulfuss und Armbruster, 1815. (Foyle–Montefiore Collection/ Müller Library: Mont 58Cb25)

Levison, George, *see* Levison, Gumperz

Levison, Gumperz, *Ma'amar ha-Torah veha-hokhmah, helek rishon*, London: 531 (1770–71). (Foyle–Montefiore Collection/Müller Library: Mont 62g15) FIGURE 11

Lindau, Barukh, 'Toldot ha-minim ha-tiv'iyim', in *Ha-Me'asef*, Königsberg, Berlin: Orientalischen Buchdruckerei, 1788. (Gedalyah Elkoshi Collection/Müller Library) FIGURE 41

Maimon, Salomon, *Salomon Maimon's Lebensgeschichte*, Berlin: Vieweg, 1792–93. (Foyle–Montefiore Collection/Müller Library: Mont 58Ca13) FIGURE 61A
————*Sefer Ta 'alumot hokhmah*, Breslau: 547 (1787). (Bodleian Library: MS. Ol. 849) FIGURE 61B

Maimonides, Moses, *Be'ur milot ha-higayon* [...]; *'im perush Mosheh mi-Desoi*, Berlin: 544 (1783–84). (Foyle–Montefiore Collection/Müller Library: Mont 61b26) FIGURE 25
ha-Me'asef, Königsberg: Kanter 546 (1785–86). (Gedalyah Elkoshi Collection/Müller Library) FIGURE 40
————Königsberg: Kanter, le-hodesh Adar I 546 (1786). (Gedalyah Elkoshi Collection/Müller Library) FIGURE 42
————Königsberg: Kanter, le-hodesh Av 546 (1786). (Gedalyah Elkoshi Collection/ Müller Library) FIGURE 43
————Königsberg: Kanter, le-hodesh Nisan 546 (1786). (Gedalyah Elkoshi Collection/Müller Library) FIGURE 44
————Berlin: Hevrat hinukh ne'arim, le-hodesh Nisan 546 (1786). (Gedalyah Elkoshi Collection/Müller Library) FIGURE 83

Mendelssohn, Moses, *Abhandlung über die Evidenz metaphysischen Wissenschaften* [...]: *nebst noch einer Abhandlung über dieselbe Materie, welche die Academie nächst der ersten für die beste gehalten hat*, Berlin: Haude und Spener, 1764. (Foyle–Montefiore Collection/Müller Library: Mont 62h7) FIGURE 19
————*Jerusalem oder überreligiöse* [*sic*] *Macht und Judenthum*, Frankfurt, Leipzig: 1791. (Foyle–Montefiore Collection/Müller Library: Mont 58Bc16) FIGURE p. x.
————*Megilat Kohelet: 'im be'ur katsar* [...], Berlin: 530 (1769–70). (Foyle–Montefiore Collection/Müller Library: Mont 61b45) FIGURES 29 & 30
———— *Morgenstunden, oder Vorlesungen über das Daseyn Gottes: erster Theil*, Frankfurt, Leipzig: 1786. (Foyle–Montefiore Collection/Müller Library: Mont 58Bd1) FIGURE 37
———— *Or li-netivah: ve-hu hakdamah le-hibur netivot ha-shalom*, Berlin: [1783]. (Foyle–Montefiore Collection/Müller Library: Mont 63b17) FIGURE 27
————*Phaedon oder über die Unsterblichkeit der Seele in drey Gesprächen*, Berlin: Nicolai, 1767. (Foyle–Montefiore Collection/Müller Library: Mont 58Bc17) FIGURE 22
————*Fedone: O dell'immortalità dell'anima; in tre dialoghi* [...], *tradotto* [...] *da Carlo Ferdinandi*, Coira: Otto, 1773. (Foyle–Montefiore Collection/Müller Library: Mont 61b41) FIGURE 23
————*Fedon: hu sefer hash'arat ha-nefesh / (le-)Mosheh mi-Desoi ha-nikra Mendelszohn;* [...] *mi-sefat Ashkenazit R. Yishai Ber*, Berlin: 547 (1786–87). (Foyle–Montefiore Collection/Müller Library: Mont 58Bc18) FIGURE 24
———— (Übersetzer), *Die Psalmen*, Berlin: Maurer, 1783. (Foyle–Montefiore Collection/Müller Library: Mont 58g16) FIGURE 28
———— *Schreiben an den Herrn Diaconus Lavater zu Zürich*, Berlin: Nicolai, 1770. (Foyle–Montefiore Collection/Müller Library: Mont 60h17) FIGURE 32

———'Ueber die Frage: was heist aufklären?', in *Berlinische Monatsschrift*, Berlin: Haude und Spener, December 1784, pp. 481–94. (Foyle–Montefiore Collection/ Müller Library: Mont 70e10)   FIGURE 21

Neumark, Meir ben Judah Loeb, *Tokhen ha-kadur*, 1706. (Bodleian Library: MS. Opp. 184)   FIGURES 7 & 8

Satanow, Isaac, *Helek rishon mi-Sefer ha-hizayon:* [...] *bi-melitsah hidot u-musar haskel*, Berlin: (1775). (Foyle–Montefiore Collection/Müller Library: Mont 58Bc17)   FIGURE 51

Schleiermacher, Friedrich, *Briefe bei Gelegenheit der politisch theologischen Aufgabe und des Sendschreibens jüdischer Hausväter*, Berlin: Franke, 1799. (Foyle–Montefiore Collection/Müller Library: Mont 60f59(2))   FIGURE 71

Schnaber, Mordechai Gumpel, *see* Levison, Gumperz

Teller, Wilhelm Abraham, *Beantwortung des Sendschreibens einiger Hausväter jüdischer Religion an mich den Probst Teller*, Berlin: Maurer, 1799. (Foyle–Montefiore Collection/Müller Library: Mont 60h1(2))   FIGURE 72

Treue Relation des ersten Eindrucks den das neuerlich erschienene an den Probst Teller gerichtete Sendschreiben einiger Juden auf das Publikum machte: ein Fingerzeig für die Juden, Berlin: 1799. (Foyle–Montefiore/Müller Library: Mont 60f59(5))   FIGURE 77

[Vollbeding, Johann Christoph], *Sollen sich die Christen beschneiden oder die Juden taufen lassen?: ein Versuch über den uralten Sinn und die allmäligen Umbildungen der jüdischen Volksreligion, mit Berücksichtigung des Sendschreibens jüdischer Hausväter an den Herrn Probst Teller in Berlin: Zur Verständigung und Annäherung beyder Religionsverwandten*, Berlin: Nicolai, 1800. (Foyle–Montefiore Collection/Müller Library: Mont 60f59)   FIGURE 76

Wessely, Moses, 'Ueber die Mittel, die Dänischen Staaten gegen Verringerung ihrer Münzen, den Fall ihres Wechselcourses u.s.w. zu sichern', in *Moses Wessely's Hinterlassene Schriften*, Berlin: Betsch, 1798. (Foyle–Montefiore Collection/Müller Library: Mont 58b28)   FIGURE 54

Wessely, Naphtali Herz, *Divre shalom ve-emet: li-kehal 'adat Yisra'el ha-garim be-artsot memshelet ha-kesar*, Vol. 4: *Rehovot*, Berlin: Verlag der Jüdischen Freyschule, [1785]. (Foyle–Montefiore Collection/Müller Library: Mont 58Ba11)   FIGURE 39

——— *Die Moseide in achtzehn Gesängen*, Berlin: Vieweg, 1795–(1806?). (Foyle–Montefiore Collection/Müller Library: Mont 58b8 v.1)   FIGURE 50

——— *Sefer ha-midot: ve-hu sefer musar haskel: kerekh rishon*, Berlin: Hevrat hinukh ne'arim, [1786]. (Foyle–Montefiore Collection/Müller Library: Mont 61b38)   FIGURE 47

———*Shire tif'eret: hibur kolel shemonah 'asar shirim* [...], Vol. 4, Prague: [1809–1829]. (Foyle–Montefiore Collection/Müller Library: Mont 59b1)   FIGURE 49

Wichmann, Gottfried Joachim, *Heman: über die Unsterblichkeit der Seele nach mosaischen Grundsätzen, in drey Gesprächen: Herrn Moses Mendelssohn zugeeignet*, Leipzig: Breitkopf, 1773. (Foyle–Montefiore Collection/Müller Library: Mont 61b35)   FIGURE 2

Wolfsohn-Halle, Aaron, *Avtalyon: ve-hu mavo ha-limud li-ne'are bene Yisra'el ule-kol ha-hafetsim, bi-leshon 'Ever*, Berlin: Hevrat hinukh ne'arim, 550 (1789 or 1790). (Foyle–Montefiore Collection/Müller Library)   FIGURE 48

Zweite Nachricht von dem Zustande der jüdischen Freischule in Berlin, Berlin: Hayn, 1804 (Foyle–Montefiore Collection/Müller Library: Mont Misc. X-2)   FIGURE 80

[?], *An einige Hausväter jüdischer Religion: über die vorgeschlagene Verbindung mit den protestantischen Christen / von einem Prediger in Berlin*, Berlin: Dieterici, 1799. (Foyle–Montefiore Collection/Müller Library: Mont 60f59)   FIGURE 74

Select bibliography

Altmann, Alexander, *Moses Mendelssohn*, Alabama, 1973.

Aptroot, Marion, Andreas Kennecke and Christoph Schulte (eds), *Isaac Euchel: der Kulturrevolutionär der jüdischen Aufklärung*, Hanover, 2010.

Bourel, Dominique, *Moses Mendelssohn et la Naissance du judaïsme moderne*, Paris, 2004.

Brann, Ross, and Adam Sutcliffe (eds), *Renewing the Past, Reconfiguring Jewish Culture: From al-Andalus to the Haskalah*, Philadelphia, 2004.

Breuer, Edward, *The Limits of Enlightenment, Jews, Germans, and the Eighteenth-Century Study of Scripture*, Cambridge MA and London, 1996.

Davies, Martin L., *Identity or History? Marcus Herz and the End of the Enlightenment*, Detroit, 1995.

Dubin, Lois C., *The Port Jews of Habsburg Trieste: Absolutist Politics and Enlightenment Culture*, Stanford CA, 1999.

Feiner, Shmuel, *Haskalah and History: The Emergence of a Modern Jewish Historical Consciousness*, Portland OR, 2002.

———*The Jewish Enlightenment*, Philadelphia, 2004.

——— and David J. Sorkin (eds), *New Perspectives on the Haskalah*, London and Portland OR, 2001.

———*The Origins of Jewish Secularization in Eighteenth-Century Europe*, Philadelphia, 2010.

———*Moses Mendelssohn, Sage of Modernity*, New Haven CT and London, 2010.

Fishman, David E., *Russia's First Modern Jews: The Jews of Shklov*, New York, 1995.

Fontaine, Resianne, Andrea Schatz and Irene Zwiep (eds), *Sepharad in Ashkenaz: Medieval Knowledge and Eighteenth-Century Enlightened Jewish Discourse*, Amsterdam, 2007.

Friedländer, David, Friedrich Schleiermacher and Wilhelm Abraham Teller, *A Debate on Jewish Emancipation and Christian Theology in Old Berlin*, ed. and trans. Richard Crouter and Julie Klassen, Indianapolis, 2004.

Hecht, Louise, *Ein jüdischer Aufklärer in Böhmen: der Pädagoge und Reformer Peter Beer (1758–1838)*, Cologne, Weimar and Vienna, 2008.

Hess, Jonathan M., *Germans, Jews, and the Claims of Modernity*, New Haven CT, 2002.

Katz, Jacob, *Out of the Ghetto: The Social Background of Jewish Emancipation*, Cambridge, 1973.

Lowenstein, Steven M., *The Berlin Jewish Community: Enlightenment, Family and Crisis, 1770–1830*, New York, 1994.

Kennecke, Andreas, *Isaac Euchel: Architekt der Haskala*, Göttingen, 2007.

Liberles, Robert, 'Dohm's Treatise on the Jews: A Defense of the Enlightenment', *Leo Baeck Institute Yearbook* 33, 1988, pp. 29–42.

Lohmann, Uta, '"Sustenance for the Learned Soul": The History of the Oriental Printing Press at the Publishing House of the Jewish Free School in Berlin', *Leo Baeck Institute Year Book* 51, 2006, pp. 11–40.

Meyer, Michael A., *The Origins of the Modern Jew: Jewish Identity and European Culture in Germany, 1749–1824*, Detroit, 1979.

Naimark-Goldberg, Natalie, 'Reading and Modernization: The Experience of Jewish Women in Berlin around 1800', *Nashim: A Journal of Jewish Women's Studies and Gender Issues* 15, Spring 2008, pp. 58–87.

———*Jewish Women in Berlin and Enlightenment Culture*, Oxford, forthcoming 2012.

Pelli, Moshe, *The Age of Haskalah, Studies in Hebrew Literature of the Enlightenment in Germany*, Leiden, 1979.

Ruderman, David B., *Jewish Thought and Scientific Discovery in Early Modern Europe*, New Haven CT, 1995.

———*Jewish Enlightenment in an English Key, Anglo-Jewry's Construction of Modern Jewish Thought*, Princeton NJ and Oxford, 2000.

——— *Early Modern Jewry: A New Cultural History*, Princeton NJ and Oxford, 2010.

Ruderman, David B. and Shmuel Feiner (eds), 'Early Modern Culture and Haskalah: Reconsidering the Borderlines of Modern Jewish History', in *Jahrbuch des Simon-Dubnow-Instituts* VI, 2007, pp. 213–96.

Sadowski, Dirk, *Haskala und Lebenwelt, Herz Homberg und die jüdischen deutschen Schulen in Galizien 1782–1806*, Göttingen, 2010.

Schatz, Andrea, *Sprache in der Zerstreuung: die Säkularisierung des Hebräischen im 18. Jahrhundert*, Göttingen, 2009.

Schulte, Christoph, *Die jüdische Aufklärung. Philosophie, Religion, Geschichte*, Munich, 2002.

Shavit, Zohar, '1779, David Friedlaender and Moses Mendelssohn publish the *Lesebuch fuer juedische Kinder*', in *Yale Companion to Jewish Writing and Thought in German Culture 1096–1996*, New Haven CT and London: 1997, pp. 68–74.

Shear, Adam, *The Kuzari and the Shaping of Jewish Identity, 1167–1900*, Cambridge, 2008.

Socher, Abraham P., *The Radical Enlightenment of Solomon Maimon: Judaism, Heresy, and Philosophy*, Stanford CA, 2006.

Sorkin, David J., *Moses Mendelssohn and the Religious Enlightenment*, Berkeley CA, 1996.

——— *The Berlin Haskalah and German Religious Thought*, London and Portland OR, 2000.

——— *The Religious Enlightenment, Protestants, Jews, and Catholics from London to Vienna*, Princeton NJ and Oxford, 2008.

Sutcliffe, Adam, *Judaism and Enlightenment*, Cambridge, 2003.